Channel
Islands

Travel Publications

CONTENTS

INTRODUCTION

For many people the name of the Channel Islands conjures up a northern mini paradise providing a tax haven for the very rich or sun and sand for the carefree holiday-maker. Although the Channel Islands have been associated with the English crown since the Norman conquest, they lie much nearer to the French coast and were largely French-speaking until the 20C. Beneath their apparent Englishness lie a thousand years of Norman tradition and sturdy independence. Under self-government the Channel Islands have fostered a most attractive relaxed atmosphere.

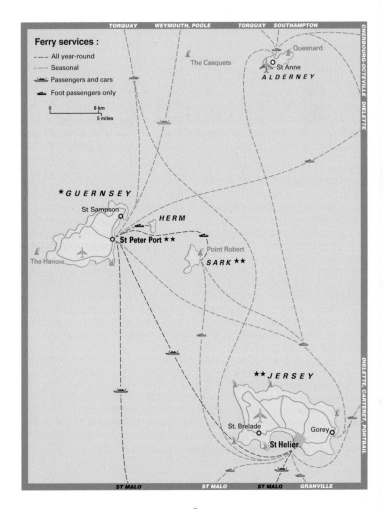

Ferry services :

- – – All year-round
- – – Seasonal
- Passengers and cars
- Foot passengers only

0   8 km
5 miles

TORQUAY   WEYMOUTH, POOLE   TORQUAY   SOUTHAMPTON

CHERBOURG-OCTEVILLE   DIELETTE

Quesnard
The Casquets
St Anne
ALDERNEY

★GUERNSEY
St Sampson
HERM
St Peter Port ★★
Point Robert
The Hanois
SARK ★★

★★JERSEY
St. Brelade
Gorey
St Helier

DIELETTE, CARTERET, PORTBAIL

ST MALO   ST MALO   ST MALO   GRANVILLE

Owing to their situation and the Gulf Stream, the islands enjoy a mild climate that nurtures spring flowers and semi-tropical plants. Local features echo not only Normandy but also Cornwall; long sandy beaches contrast with rugged cliffs; quiet country lanes meander between traditional granite houses. Tidal currents in the islands are among the strongest in the world; at low water, when the sea may retreat as much as 40ft/12m, huge areas of rocky reefs are exposed, greatly increasing the land mass and making it possible to walk seaward (up to 2mi/3km). All the islands encourage and control tourism, constructing marinas to attract sailors, ensuring clean beaches for surfers and swimmers, and conserving the countryside to the delight of bird-watchers, walkers and cyclists.

■ Geography and Location

The Channel Islands lie to the north of the Gulf of St Malo, and to the west of the Cherbourg peninsula. Alderney is the northernmost, located some 80mi/128km south of Weymouth, on the south coast of England, and 9mi/14.5km from the Breton coast. Sail south for 21mi/36km and you would reach Guernsey, Herm and Sark. From here it is another 21mi/36km to Jersey. Continue south again and, after 44mi/70km you would reach land near the Breton port of St Malo.

The seas surrounding the islands are subject to some of the biggest tidal movements in the world – during the spring tides, the water can rise at a rate of 2in/5cm per minute, varying by as much as 40ft/12m between low and high tide. This effect is visible in the vast swathes of golden sand that are exposed at low tide and in the acres of weed-covered rock that appear on all sides. These rocks are a great hazard to shipping, and beachcombers need to be constantly aware of the tides as they explore the crab-filled rock-pools of the foreshore. Check low water times and venture out only in the two hours before and after.

The Channel Islands are divided into two groups, called Bailiwicks, for administrative purposes, and they have a combined population of around 140 000 – the same number of inhabitants as the Isle of Wight, but with just half the land area – 75sq mi/194km^2 in total.

The Bailiwick of Jersey

The Bailiwick of Jersey consists of Jersey itself, and the rocky islets of Ecréhous and the Minquiers Reeg (also known as The Minkies). Measuring 9mi/14.5km east to west and 5mi/8km north to south, Jersey is the biggest of the islands (population 80 000) and the most southerly (lying 100 miles south of mainland Britain). Much of the island is composed of pink and grey granite, which provides the island with an excellent and durable building material. The granite weathers to form a free-draining soil whose fertility has been enhanced over many centuries by the lavish use of *vraic* (seaweed) as a fertiliser, a practice that continues to this day. From the dramatic cliffs at the northern edge of the island to the golden beaches of the south, Jersey tilts towards the southerly sun like a giant solar panel. Farmers have long taken advantage of the sun-trap effect to produce early-season crops of the famous Jersey Royal potatoes.

The Bailiwick of Guernsey

The Bailiwick of Guernsey consists of the islands of Guernsey, Alderney, Sark, Herm and Jethou, along with the lighthouse rocks of the Casquests, and the uninhabited islets of Burhou and Ortac. **Guernsey** (population 60 000) is the second-largest of the Channel Islands, roughly triangular in shape and measuring around 7mi/11km wide and 9mi/14.5km deep. Charming **Sark** (3mi/5km wide by 1mi/1.6km deep) has a

population of 600, greatly swelled by summer visitors arriving on day trips from Guernsey, 9mi/14.5km to the west. **Herm** (1.5mi/2.5km by 0.75mi/1km, population 103) is even closer to Guernsey: thousands of holidaymakers every year make the short 20-minute journey from St Peter Port to the island's tiny harbour. **Alderney** (population 2 000) is the third largest of the islands (3.5mi/5.6km long by 1mi/1.6km wide) and the most northerly; most of its summer visitors come over from France, since the island lies a mere 9mi/14.5 km from the Cotentin peninsula.

■ History
Prehistory
The remains of some of Europe's earliest people have been found at the internationally important site of La Cotte de St Brelade, on Jersey's southwest coast.

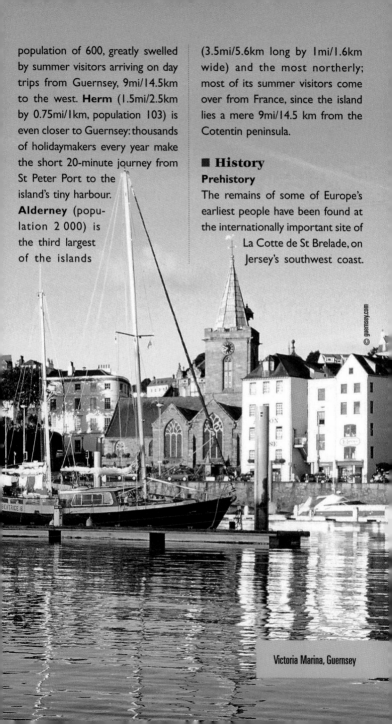

© guernsey.com

Victoria Marina, Guernsey

The finds, now displayed in the Jersey Museum, date from a quarter of a million years ago, when Jersey was still attached to the mainland of Europe. They show that Jersey's earliest inhabitants lived in caves and had an ingenious method of survival: they herded mammoth and woolly rhino together and deliberately drove them to their death over the cliffs, eating the flesh and using the skins to clothe themselves.

Some 10 000 years ago, at the end of the last Ice Age, the melting ice sheet caused sea levels to rise, cutting the Channel Islands off from the continent of Europe. Jersey and Alderney remained attached to the continent for 2 000 years longer than the other islands, which is why they have animals and reptiles, such as moles and toads, that are not found on Guernsey, Herm and Sark.

By this time, our prehistoric ancestors had developed into sophisticated farmers with a highly complex social organisation. Whoever controlled the

Trepierd dolman,
Guernsey

© guernsey.com

10

islands – whether a priestly caste or warrior overlords – was certainly able to command vast resources and manpower, as the island's many passage graves demonstrate.

Traders and Saints

As the peoples of Europe became more mobile, travelling far and wide by ship to trade their goods, the Channel Islands became a frequent port of call, and one of the most exciting archaeological finds of recent years is the Gallo-Roman boat discovered in St Peter Port. Close links with the Gauls of northern France continued into the early Christian era. St Marculf came over from Brittany and converted the islands to Christianity in AD 538.

From then on, the islands looked to Brittany for their religious leadership, and many parishes (such as St Helier and St Brelade) are named after the Celtic saints and hermits who founded small monastic cells on the remote islands.

Normans and Tudors

In 933 the islands were annexed by the Normans and attached to the English Crown by William the Conqueror. All was well until 1204, when King Philippe II of France conquered Normandy. The Channel Islands remained free but faced the most decisive moment in their history – whether to stay part of Normandy, or whether to remain loyal to their 'Duke', the English King John. The people of the Channel Islands decided to stick with King John. In doing so, they gained valuable privileges, including the right of independent government. To this day, the islands

St Ouen's Manor, Jersey

remain subject only to the reigning monarch, and not to the British parliament.

Despite this, the French made repeated attempts over the centuries to regain the islands. In 1483 a Papal Bull of Neutrality was issued which remained in force until 1689. During the English Civil War Jersey upheld the Royalist cause whereas Guernsey sided with Cromwell; this is supposed to be the basis of the traditional rivalry between the two major islands. In 1649, immediately following the execution of Charles I, Jersey declared his son, Charles II, as monarch, the first place in the realm officially to do so, some 11 years before the Restoration.

The Battle of Jersey

In 1781, an invasion force, led by Baron de Rullecourt, landed in Jersey and took the Governor by surprise, persuading him that he headed a force several thousand strong. He surrendered the island, but Major Francis Peirson, at the head of the Jersey Militia, refused to accept defeat and attacked the French in Royal Square. The Battle of Jersey lasted a mere ten minutes and ended in the defeat of the French – but also the death of the gallant Major Peirson. The Battle of Jersey – the last battle ever to be fought on British soil – is widely commemorated on Jersey as a symbol of the islanders' determination to retain their independence.

At the beginning of the 19C the rise of Napoleon brought the threat of invasion and so defensive towers, similar to the later Martello and round towers, were built along the coasts. Later in the century fresh fears of French invasion brought more fortifications, particularly in Alderney.

German Occupation

The Channel Islands were finally invaded by a foreign power – by the Germans in 1940: the only British territory to fall to the enemy. This was regarded by islanders who had long pledged their loyalty to the Crown as a symbolic act by Hitler. The five years of occupation brought hardship: the people were completely isolated save for news picked up by clandestine radios; there were shortages of food and clothing and deportations to Germany. During the winter of 1944-5 the islanders and the occupier came close to starvation for, although the Allies

Liberation Day Cavelcade, Guernsey

had re-captured the Normandy coast, the Germans had surrendered St Malo, the port they used to supply the Channel Islands, and the British Liberation Task Force 135 did not arrive until 9 May 1945. During the occupation massive concrete fortifications, some of which are still visible, were constructed, as part of Hitler's impregnable Atlantic Wall, by the slave labour of the Todt Organisation. In fact, they were never tested, simply by-passed by the

Clameur de Haro

The ancient legal remedy which is still in force is thought to invoke Rollo, a 10C Norse chieftain. A victim of wrongdoing must kneel down in the presence of two witnesses and say *"Haro, haro, haro, à l'aide, mon Prince, on me fait tort"* (Help, my Prince, someone is doing me wrong). This must be followed by the recital of the Lord's Prayer in French. The wrongdoer must then desist until a court ruling has been obtained.

Normandy landings. During this time there were many acts of bravery and heroism, and accusations of collaboration, which have left unhealed scars among those who lived through the war. Most have learned to forgive and forget, however, and the Channel Islands now attract many German, as well as French and British visitors, who come specifically to visit the islands' many war-time relics.

After the war, the potato industry recovered quickly. The Jersey Royal Kidney Fluke, developed more than 100 years ago and unique to the island, is now worth £24 millions a year in exports to the UK alone. In the 1940s and 1950s, unemployed French labourers were imported annually from Brittany to take part in the labour-intensive potato harvest, and, since the 1960s, their place has been taken by Portuguese workers from Madeira and the mainland. Today's large population of Portuguese mostly work in the hotel and catering industry, as agriculture has become increas-ingly mechanised, and tourism and financial services have taken over as the mainstays of the island economies.

■ Economy

Until the 18C fishing and agriculture were the main activities. In the Middle Ages large quantities of cod and conger eel were exported to England and Normandy to be eaten on the many days in the medieval church calendar when meat was forbidden. The fish were split and dried on small sticks *(perches)* in remote places: the smell was reported as being most unpleasant. The trade died when the Newfoundland fisheries were established in the 16C but the practice is recalled in *eperquerie*, a common place name in the Channel Islands. In the past the **ormer** or sea ear *(oreille de mer)* was a local delicacy prepared by stewing or pickling after being well beaten to make it tender. The shell is lined with mother-of-pearl and sometimes contains pearls. This mollusc is now rare and fishing is banned in all the islands but ormers are farmed on Guernsey. Following heavy storms, seaweed (*vraic* – pronounced "rack") was collected from the beaches to be used as fertiliser and fuel. Large flocks of sheep were kept on the higher exposed ground; indeed the words Jersey and Guernsey have entered the English language to mean woollen cloth or a woollen garment; in the 17C people engaged in knitting were known to neglect the harvest.

In the 18C huge fortunes were made from privateering under Letters of Marque and ship-building flourished. In the 19C granite was exported in vast quantities for road-making and construction work. Cattle too, usually known on the mainland as "Alderneys" – probably because this was the last port of call for ships returning to Poole or Southampton – came to be in great demand for the high butter-fat content of their milk; now only Jerseys and Guernseys are pure-bred.

Channel Island Cattle

The distinctive petite Jersey cow, with its long-lashed doe-eyes, its black muzzle and pale biscuit-colour, is largely the result of a careful breeding programme undertaken by Colonel John Le Couteur in the 1830s, after the importation of foreign stock was banned in 1789. In 1866 a herd book was started listing by name the animals which were selected on the basis of their looks and high milk yield, so rich in butterfat. The darker-coloured bulls are less docile creatures. In winter Jersey cattle are often protected from the cold by special woollen coats.

The Guernsey cow, which is heftier than the Jersey, varies in colour from a pale honey colour to a dark red; the head is distinguished by a pink muzzle and, occasionally, by a white blaze. During the summer when the cows are put out to pasture, the milk is a distinctive yellow colour. Cross-breeding with imported strains ensures faster production for beef stock only; the true Guernsey bloodstock has been contained since 1819. Cattle may still be seen in fields tethered to a post by a chain around the horns; this is an economical way of controlling grazing but very labour-intensive, as the animals have to be watered regularly.

Farming still plays a role in the local economy, supplying local markets and the British mainland with early vegetables (potatoes, tomatoes, grapes) and cut flowers.

Since the end of the Second World War, the Channel Islands have taken advantage of their sunny climate and their status as self-governing Crown dependencies to develop tourism and international financial services, which now provide the major part of their income. Under stable government and low rates of personal and corporate taxation, the larger islands have developed a buoyant industry in **international financial services**, including off-shore banking, trust management and insurance, which are strictly regulated. Additional income, although small, is generated by international collectors of the highly decorative special issues of stamps and of coinage; coins, bank-notes and postage stamps are issued locally but are not legal tender elsewhere.

■ People and Culture

The Channel Islands have a legacy of tradition arising from their Anglo-Norman history. They owe their ultimate loyalty to the Duke of Normandy, the title by which they know the reigning monarch of England. When Channel Islanders drink a loyal toast, they raise their glasses to 'The Queen, Our Duke'.

Ice cream vendor, Sark

© guernsey.com

DAIRY MARY MAID

SARK ICE CREAM

The Only **SARK** DAIRY ICE CREAM

Internal affairs are managed by the two island parliaments, known as the States Assembly, though the islands delegate to the Home Office in London decisions relating to defence and international affairs. The Assemblies are made up of elected senators and deputies, and the islands take a certain pride in reaching consensus decisions, proudly boasting that they have no political parties, prime minister or cabinet.

Despite their similarities, there is a great deal of rivalry between Jersey and Guernsey. Guernsey markets itself as the 'friendly island', with the unspoken implication that people on Jersey are a bit hard-bitten and citified. Each of the Bailiwicks has its own currency and its own incompatible phone cards, not to mention its own postage stamps and different coloured letter-boxes and phone booths. Only half in jest will you hear Jerseymen referred to as *crapauds* (toads) — because the toad is found in Jersey and but not in Guernsey; returning the compliment, Guernseymen, with their slower pace of life, are dismissed as *ânes* (donkeys) by their bigger island rivals.

In architecture, there are strong similarities between the islands, with many fine granite farmhouses dating from the 17C and 18C. Datestones above the main doorways are sometimes deceptive: it was traditional for newlyweds to have their initials and the date carved on the lintel stone, but the house itself may well be much older. Manor houses, one to each of the island parishes, can be distinguished from other wealthy properties by the presence of a colombier, or dovecote, such as the one at Hamptonne Country Life Museum (see Index). Only manorial seigneurs were allowed to keep pigeons – feeding freely on their tenants' crops!

Today, wealth and privilege are signalled by the ownership of luxury cars, of shich there are many on the two larger islands, despite speed limits which mean that they will never be tested to their full potential. With income tax at only 20 per cent, and no capital taxes at all, the islands attract many wealthy residents, of whom TV traveller Alan Whicker, writer Jack Higgins (author of The Eagle Has Landed and 15 other best-sellers), and actor John Nettles, star of TV's Bergerac and Midsomer Murders, are among the better known.

Strict limits are set on the number of residency permits granted, however, and the islanders are very conscious of the need not to swamp the islands with houses, which would only destroy the features that make the Channel Islands so appealing. One of these is the intricate network of rural 'Green Lanes' that criss-cross both islands, providing an escape route for horse-riders, walkers and cyclists from the busier main roads. Also designed for escape – quite literally – are the ancient sanctuary paths (perquage) that run from the parish church to the sea: those who took sanctuary in the church were escorted down these paths to a waiting boat and were given help so long as they swore to leave the island for ever.

Exploring these lanes is a good way to discover the rich wildlife of the islands, where chemical-free farming has allowed wild flowers to flourish, along with many species of butterflies and birds. The islands combine northern European flora and fauna with such Mediterranean species as the green lizard, plus some creatures that are unique to the islands, such as the Jersey black vole.

■ Religion

Christianity seems to have been introduced in the 6C by Celtic saints from Brittany, Cornwall and Wales. Originally the parishes were attached to the diocese of Coutances in Normandy and remained so until Elizabeth I transferred them to the See of Winchester in 1568.

At the Reformation, **Calvinism** (Reformed Protestantism) took hold, a natural choice given the linguistic links with France, boosted by the influx of Huguenot refugees fleeing persecution on the Continent. **Anglicanism** was eventually introduced at the Restoration in 1660 but the English language was not used for church services until this century. **Methodism** was preached in the islands by John Wesley himself and has always had a strong following, particularly in Guernsey.

■ Language

English is now the universal language of the islands; the native tongue, a dialect of Norman-French, the language of William the Conqueror, is rarely spoken. In Jersey and Guernsey, societies for its preservation exist which trace the regional variations in vocabulary and pronunciation. In Jersey the dialect is called Jerriais and those who speak it are called Jersiais. French survives in many areas of Channel Islands life – especially in legal and government affairs. The names of long-established island families are French, and the street names are bilingual (often a street name with a very prosaic English name will have a far more descriptive French alternative – High Street, for example, is La Rue des Trois Pigeons in French, referring to an inn of the same name that once stood there).

© Jersey.com

Aerial view of Seymour Tower, Jersey

■ Wrecks and Lighthouses

The Channel Islands are surrounded by extensive offshore reefs and rocky islets. The coast, together with strong tides, treacherous currents and fog, make these seas some of the most hazardous in Britain, claiming many ships. Among those documented are a Roman galley which sank off St Peter Port; the *White Ship* carrying the heir to the English throne which foundered on the Casquets in 1119; *HMS Victory*, which went down on the Casquets in 1774 with the loss of 1 000 men; the *Liverpool*, the largest sailing ship wrecked in the Channel Islands, which ran aground off Corblets Bay in a fog in 1902; the *Briseis*, which struck a reef off Vazon Bay in 1937 with 7 000 casks of wine on board; the *Orion*, an oil rig mounted on an ocean-going barge, which ran aground off Grand Rocques in Guernsey in 1978. There are now four lighthouses owned by Trinity House in the Channel Islands.

The earliest to be built was the one marking the **Casquets** (1723); then followed the three towers, known as St Peter, St Thomas and Donjon (30ft high), which were lit by coal fires. In 1770 oil lamps were introduced, and in 1818 revolving lights which had to be wound every two hours. The main light (120ft above sea-level) now has a range of 17mi in clear weather. The story of the lightkeeper's daughter, who found life on Alderney too noisy, is beautifully told by Swinburne in his poem *Les Casquettes*.

The **Hanois Lighthouse** was built in 1862 on the treacherous Hanois Reef. The first approaches for a light were made to Trinity House in 1816 but 43 years passed before the decision to build was taken. The tower (117ft above sea-level; 32ft in diameter) is constructed of Cornish granite.

Quesnard Light (1912) on Alderney and **Point Robert** (1913) on Sark are sited on land rather than offshore and can be visited. Point Robert is most unusual in that the light is mounted above the buildings for stores and accommodation which cling to the cliff face like a Greek monastery. ■

Lillie Langtry – the Jersey Lily

Lillie Langtry, the vivacious and beautiful daughter of the Dean of Jersey, was born in St Saviour's parish in 1853. Having visited London as an 18th birthday treat, she resolved to escape Jersey, agreeing to marry Edward Langtry, a man of considerable wealth – or so it seemed. His wealth turned out to be less than his extravagant lifestyle suggested, but he provided Lillie's passport to London society, where her radiant character and perfect complexion inspired the poets and painters of her day.

Her famous 1878 portrait by Sir Edward Millais is entitled *The Jersey Lily*, a pun on her name and a reference to the nerine flower that she holds in her hands. Sir Edward Poynter's more sensuous portrait, of Lillie in a low-cut dress of gorgeous red and gold, perhaps captures better the coquettish nature that enabled her to embark on a three-year affair with the Prince of Wales. Invited to every party, Lillie became one of London's Professional Beauties, her picture appearing daily in newspapers and magazines, and her taste in clothes setting the style that other women followed.

Lillie's life changed dramatically when the Prince of Wales turned against her, following a misjudged prank (Lillie dropped an ice-cream down his back at a ball, which the Prince interpreted as contempt for his person). Lillie was suddenly shunned by society, debts were called in and she was bankrupted. Friends persuaded her to go on the stage, where she quickly rebuilt her wealth. Her career took her to the US where the New York Times railed against her lack of propriety in 'going beyond the bounds of good taste in unnecessarily removing her clothes on stage'. Despite, or perhaps because of, this, she enjoyed an immensely successful career, even starring in a silent movie in 1913, before retiring to a secluded life in Monte Carlo.

Subsequent commentators have hailed Lillie Langtry as a pioneer of the right of women to lead an independent and unshackled life. Another perspective is provided by Ira Goldsmith, her secretary and companion, who called Lillie 'the saddest woman I have ever known – loaded with jewels and famous, yet many a night I have known her cry herself to sleep'.

SIGHTS

JERSEY★★

Population 85 150
Michelin Atlas p 5 or Map 503

Jersey is the largest of the Channel Islands (45sq mi/116km²; 9×5mi); it lies close to the coast of France (12mi/19km). It is more or less rectangular and slopes gently from the north coast with its dramatic steep pink-granite cliffs (300–400ft), opening here and there into a sandy bay or plunging into the sea, to the couth coast with its firm flat sandy beaches interspersed with rocky outcrops.

Victor Hugo, who spent three years in Jersey (1852-55) before moving to Guernsey, was enchanted: "It possesses a unique and exquisite beauty. It is a garden of flowers cradled by the sea. Woods, meadows and gardens seem to mingle with the rocks and reefs in the sea."

The island is ringed by several circular defensive towers, built in the 18C and 19C and similar to the Martello towers on the south coast of England.

In addition to the delights of the beaches and the countryside, visitors to Jersey can enjoy a wide range of more sophisticated pleasures – theatre and cinema, cabaret and floor shows, discotheques and discobars.

Economy – Agriculture has long sustained the islanders: wheat and rye, turnips and parsnips, four-horned sheep supplying wool for

© Jersey.com

Mont Orgueil castle

Practical Information

Visitor Services Centre – www.jersey.com

Liberation Square, St Helier, Jersey JE1 1BB ☏ 01534 500 777; ☏ 01534 500 888 (Jerseylink Accommodation); Fax 01534 500 808; info@jersey.com

Jersey Tourism Office, 7 Lower Grosvenor Place, London SW1W 0EN, ☏ 020 7233 7474; Fax 020 7630 0747.

Where to Stay – There are approximately 200 hotels and guest houses as well as self-catering premises and registered camp sites. See the Practical Information chapter for suggestions on where to stay.

Access – By air or sea from the mainland. See p 111.

Jersey Airport – ☏ 01534 49 09 99.

Motoring – Visitors may bring their own vehicles (maximum width 7ft 6.5in). If they wish to hire a car, they must be over 21 and have a valid driving licence with no endorsements for dangerous or drunken driving in the previous 5 years.

Parking in municipal parking spaces or car parks is payable by scratch cards or clock discs, which are on sale from newsagents. Parking is free of charge from Monday to Saturday, between 5pm and 8am, and all day on Sundays and Bank Holidays.

Highway Code – **Seat-belts** must be worn at all times. **Children** under the age of 14 must travel in the rear of the car.

A **yellow line** painted across the road at a junction serves as a STOP or HALT sign and requires drivers to stop before emerging onto the major road.

A **yellow grid** at an intersection requires drivers not to enter the box unless their way ahead is clear.

Filter in turn at roundabouts requires drivers to give way to the first car from the right before entering onto the roundabout themselves.

The **speed limit** in Jersey is 40mph on open roads, 30mph in built-up areas, 20mph where indicated and 15mph in Green Lanes or where indicated.

All **accidents** involving any vehicle should be reported to a policeman (in uniform or honorary: ask a local person); vehicles should not be moved from the scene before the incident has been reported.

Cycle Hire – Motorcycles and mopeds are hired to people of 21 or over, although some companies may hire mopeds to 18 and over. Baby seats are usually available with rented bicycles.

Taxis – There are taxi ranks at the airport and in St Helier. Tariffs vary for day and night and on public holidays; extra charges are made for waiting time and luggage not carried in the passenger compartment.

Buses – Buses operate throughout the island, including the Airport, from the Bus Station at the Weighbridge in St Helier (☎ 01534 721 201); explorer tickets are available for 7-day, 5-day, 3-day and 1-day excursions.

Boat trips – Day trips to Guernsey, Sark, Herm and France are organised by Trident Tours, The Ferry Centre, 5 The Esplanade ☎ 01534 726 452. Coastal cruises are provided by South Coast Cruises, Albert Quay, St Helier ☎ 01534 732 466; Fax 01534 789 465.

Shopping – The minimal duty levied on imported luxury items makes shopping an attractive activity – jewellery, gold and silver work, pearls, and a variety of crafts (pottery, candles).

Most shops and businesses in St Helier open from Monday to Saturday; the indoor markets in St Helier close on Thursday afternoons.

When buying home-grown produce offered for sale by the roadside, place the money in the honesty box.

Licensed premises – Public bars may open to adults (over 18) from 9am (11am Sundays) to 11pm; children under 18 are permitted in public bars until 9pm if accompanied by an adult.

Festivals – Jersey offers the annual **world famous Battle of Flowers**, the **International Food Festival** and the **International Air Rally**, as well as several **walking festivals**, a **cycling festival** and a multitude of festivals and events celebrating the nature and heritage of the island.

Beaches – There are several facilities for water-skiing, windsurfing, surfing, sub-squa diving, sailing, canoeing, surf jets etc. The island beaches excel in terms of cleanliness; all dogs must be kept on leads on the beaches in summer (May-Sep, 10.30am- 6pm) and all waste disposed of hygienically.

There are patrolled beaches at St Brelade's Bay, St Ouen's Bay and Plémont Bay (west coast). It is safest to bathe between the bi-coloured red and yellow flags which mark the patrolled areas; a plain red flag indicates that conditions are dangerous.

The beaches of the **southwest coast** are sheltered from the heavy Atlantic swell; St Ouen's Bay on the **west coast** presents a superb long stretch of firm sand. On the **north coast**, probably the most dramatic, there are a few sandy bays flanked by steep pink-granite cliffs (300–400ft).

Beware of the Spring tides which involve the greatest variation between high and low water (max 40ft/12m) and of being cut off by an incoming tide. Tide tables are published daily in the local newpapers and lists are available at tackle shops and newsagents.

Walking - Jersey has a network of over 45mi/72km of "Green Lanes", quiet country lanes which have a speed limit of 15mph and give priority to walkers, cyclists and horse riders. Jersey also offers 15mi/24km of coastal footpaths stretching along the north coast. Free guided walks, organised by Jersey Tourism, exploring all areas of the island, are available throughout the year.

Cycling - Jersey has 350mi/563km of roads, by-ways and lanes and a signed cycle network (96mi/155km). Maps and guides, specially designed by local cyclists, feature recommended routes and itineraries, refreshment stops, historic sites and attractions. Free guided tours are also available.

Wildlife – In sheltered spots the cliffs in the south-west provide a haven for plants – ox-eye daisies, thrift, sea campion, sheep's bit scabious, spotted rock-roses. The landward side of the west coast road is a conservation area where green lizards bask among hundreds of different plants, while kestrels and skylarks watch from the sky. The cliff paths along the north coast are crowded with wild flowers which attract a profusion of butterflies.

Bird-watching – The sparsely populated north coast is frequented by sea-birds such as fulmar, petrel, shag, lesser and great black-backed gulls, herring gulls and the occasional puffin. The species to be seen elsewhere include gulls, shags, oystercatchers and ravens.

Fishing – The continental shelf along the **eastern coast** is shallow so that at low tide, the sands and rocks are warmed by the sun and attract feeding bass and mullet as the water returns (St Catherine's Bay, Royal Bay of Grouville and St Clement's Bay). The **southwest coast** is blessed with beaches which are good for fishing (garfish, grey mullet, pollack, wrasse, conger, bass and mackerel). On the **west coast** fish, notably bass and wrasse, are swept in from the open sea by the tides and currents onto a long stretch of firm sand beach (St Ouen's Bay) flanked by rocky outcrops. The deep water off the **north coast** is good for wrasse, bass, garfish, black bream and conger.

Local specialities – Among the mouth-watering displays of seafood one may find **Bean Crock**, a dish of beans and pigs trotters; **Conger Eel soup** garnished with marigold flower petals; des **boudelots**, apples baked in a spicy dough and des **Mervelles** (also known as **Jersey Wonders**), a deep-fried doughnut-type cake. In November it may be possible to taste **Black Butter**, a preserve made by long boiling (16hr) of cider, apples and spices in a large copper pot (*bachin*).

the famous Jersey stockings and knitwear (17C), apples for cider (18C), eating grapes grown under glass and famous Doyenne de Comice pears. The mild climate continues to favour the cultivation of flowers (daffodils, freesias, carnations and lavender) and vegetables for export (potatoes including the famous Jersey Royal, cabbages, broccoli and tomatoes which became more lucrative than apples). Some crops are grown in the open fields, others under glass. Unique to Jersey is the giant cabbage *(Brassica oleracea longata)* which grows up to 10ft tall.

As traditional industries such as boat building, knitting and fishing have dwindled, more lucrative businesses have developed in tourism and financial services, industries which sustain the highly competitive young residents who have benefited from excellent local education.

Historical notes – The tombs and prehistoric monuments found on the island indicate human habitation

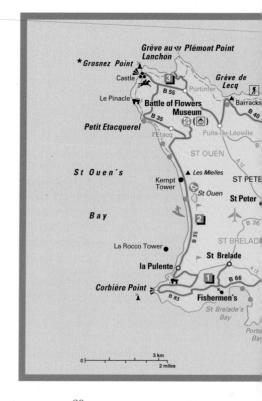

between 7500 and 2500 BC. The Roman presence was brief, and in the 6C St Helier arrived and established Christianity. The dominant influence is that of the Normans who invaded the islands in the 10C and left a rich heritage of customs and traditions that survive even today.

After 1204, when King John was forced to cede Normandy to France, the French made repeated attempts to recover the Channel Islands: the last attempt occurred in 1781 when Baron de Rullecourt, a soldier of fortune, landed by night in St Clement's Bay in the southeast corner of Jersey. Taken by surprise the Lt Governor surrendered but under Major Peirson, a young man of 24, the militia and British forces engaged the enemy and defeated them in the main square in what came to be known as the **Battle of Jersey**; both leaders were mortally wounded.

Constitution – Jersey is divided into 12 Parishes, which together with two groups of islets, the Minquiers to the south and the

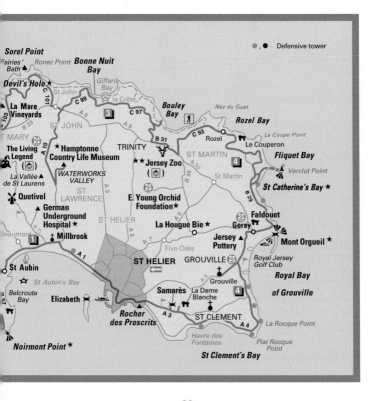

Ecréhous to the northeast, make up the Bailiwick of Jersey. The parliament, known as the States of Jersey, is headed by five officers: the Lt Governor, normally a high-ranking military man who represents the Queen; the Bailiff, a senior judge who acts as President of the States; the Attorney-General and the Solicitor-General who contribute to debates in Parliament in a consultative capacity only – these four officers are appointed by the Crown – the fifth officer is the Dean of Jersey, an Anglican clergyman. Together, they preside over 12 Senators, 12 Constables and 29 Deputies, elected to serve for a period of three to six years – all of whom assume different functions on the different committees.

■ St Helier

St Helier is a lively town, the main commercial centre on the island and the seat of government, situated in a sheltered position on the south side of the island. The shops in the pedestrian precinct formed by **King and Queen Streets** are a popular attraction for visitors to the island. English street names have sometimes replaced the more evocative Norman. Church Street was formerly called Rue Trousse Cotillon where women had to tuck up their skirts out of the mire.

The town is named after St Helier, one of the first Christian missionaries to land in Jersey, who was murdered by pirates after living as a hermit there for 15 years (c AD 555). The scant local population was swelled by two waves

Famous sons and daughters

The most famous name connected with Jersey is **Lillie Langtry** (1853-1929) – the "Jersey Lily" who became an actress and a close friend of Edward VII and captivated British high society with her beauty – she is buried in St Saviour's churchyard.

The fashionable 19C painter, **Sir John Everett Millais** (1829-96) who won acclaim with his painting entitled *Bubbles*, grew up in Jersey and belonged to an old island family. So too did **Elinor Glyn** (1864-1943), who became a novelist and Hollywood scriptwriter.

The well-known French firm which makes Martell brandy was started by **Jean Martell** from St Brelade.

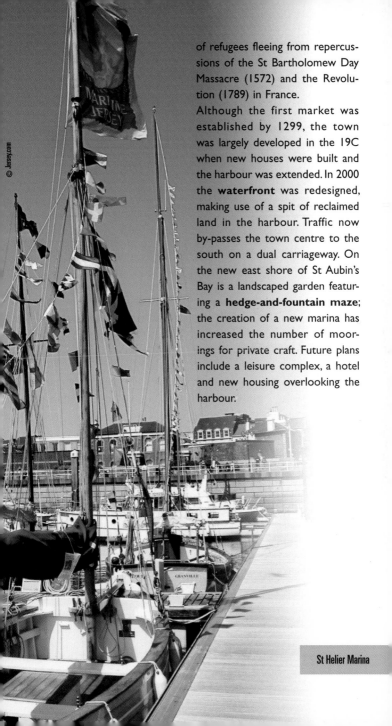

of refugees fleeing from repercussions of the St Bartholomew Day Massacre (1572) and the Revolution (1789) in France.

Although the first market was established by 1299, the town was largely developed in the 19C when new houses were built and the harbour was extended. In 2000 the **waterfront** was redesigned, making use of a spit of reclaimed land in the harbour. Traffic now by-passes the town centre to the south on a dual carriageway. On the new east shore of St Aubin's Bay is a landscaped garden featuring a **hedge-and-fountain maze**; the creation of a new marina has increased the number of moorings for private craft. Future plans include a leisure complex, a hotel and new housing overlooking the harbour.

St Helier Marina

© Jersey.com

Building façade, Queen Street

St Helier Parish Church (ZR) – The foundation of the present pink-granite church with its square tower pre-dates the Conquest. It was here that Parish business was decided up until 1830 and where the militia cannon was kept until 1844. It continues to be the seat of the Dean of Jersey – hence the epithet "Cathedral of Jersey". In the south transept hangs a plan of the seating in 1868 showing the names of the pew-holders: the nearer the altar, the higher the rent. The altar cross and candlesticks were a gift from Queen Elizabeth, the Queen Mother.

Royal Square (Z20) – The gilded-lead statue of George II, dressed as a Roman emperor, looks down on this charming small square with its spreading chestnut trees; from this point are measured the distances to all the milestones on the island. It was here in the Market Place that malefactors were once exposed in the pillory during market hours and where the Battle of Jersey erupted. Bordering the south side are the granite buildings of the **Royal Court House (ZJ)**. The public entrance bears the arms of George II, the Bailiff's entrance the arms of George VI. A plaque

Vega Memorial

Near the entrance to the States Building is a monument erected to commemorate the arrival of the Red Cross ship on 30 December 1944 bringing urgent supplies for the islanders, some of whom boldly incised a "V for Victory" into the granite pavement under German gaze.

records the birth of the Norman poet, **Wace** (1135-74). At the east end of the range of buildings are the **States Chambers** (entrance round the corner) where the Jersey parliament sits in session.

Central Market (ZE) – The granite building (1882) is furnished with cast-iron grilles at the windows and entrances, and covered with a glass (perspex) roof supported on iron columns. Beneath it open stall holders proffer local produce to the sound of the fountain, which makes this a lively and colourful scene. The **fish market (ZF)** is around the corner in Beresford Street.

Jersey Museum★ (ZM²) – Housed in a former merchant's house and adjoining warehouse belonging to Philippe Nicolle (1769-1835) is the local museum which tells the story of the island, its traditions and its industries.

The **ground-floor** area is shared by temporary exhibitions and films about Jersey. The treadmill, which was turned by 12 men and operated a pepper mill, was used in St Helier prison during the 19C. By the stairs is displayed a number of silver toilet articles from the set which accompanied Lillie Langtry on her travels.

Central Market

© Jersey.com

On the **first floor**, the history of the island from the Stone Age to the present is unfurled as a series of tableaux: artefacts excavated at La Cotte; archive photographs and interactive screens complemented by historic tools and implements to illustrate traditional farming and fishing practices; the development of Jersey as a Victorian resort and as a centre offering off-shore banking and other financial services.

The **second floor** displays the Barreau-Le Maistre collection of fine art with paintings, drawings and watercolours by local artists or of topographical interest: Sir John Everett Millais PRA (1829-96), PJ Ouless

(1817-85), "the Jersey Turner" J Le Capelain (1812-48) and the illustrator Edmund Blampied (1886-1966). Works by **Sir Francis Cook** (1907-78) bequeathed to the Jersey Heritage Trust are on permanent display in their own gallery, a converted Methodist Chapel, in Augrès (A 8, La Route de Trinité).

The **third floor** rooms recreate domestic interiors (1861) typical of a middle-class Jersey family.

New North Quay (Z) – The most prominent landmark is the world's largest **steam clock (Z S)** (36ft tall), modelled on a traditional paddle-steamer of a type that once shuttled between the islands and Southampton. It was inaugurated in August 1997 as part of the development of the St Helier waterfront.

Maritime Museum and Jersey Occupation Tapestry (M³) – Installed in converted 19C warehouses, the Jersey **Maritime Museum** is dedicated to celebrating the importance of the sea with changing displays relating to the fishing, ship-building and trading industries and to piracy.

The **Jersey Occupation Tapestry** comprises 12 panels (6x3ft) illustrating the story of the Occupation of Jersey from the outbreak of war to the Liberation: each scene, based on archive photographs and contemporary film footage, has been embroidered by a separate Parish. An audio-visual presentation provides additional background information.

Fort Regent (Z) – Access by escalators in Pier Road. The massive fortifications of Fort Regent were built to protect Jersey from invasion by Napoleon. Within, topped by a shallow white dome, is a modern leisure centre providing a variety of sports facilities and entertainment: swimming pool, badminton, squash, table tennis, snooker, play area for children, puppet theatre, exhibitions, aquarium, and audio-visual shows on the history and culture of the island. It is also home to the Jersey Signal Station. The rampart walk provides splendid **views**★ of the town and St Aubin's Bay *(west)*.

Island Fortress Occupation Museum (Z M^1) – A limited collection of military uniforms, flak sheds, weaponry and equipment evoke the five-year German occupation (1940-45). A video tells of the anguish endured and of the relief of the eventual liberation.

Elizabeth Castle (Z) – *Access on foot by a causeway at low tide (30min); otherwise by amphibious vehicle from West Park Slipway.*

In the 12C William Fitz-Hamon, one of Henry II's courtiers, founded an abbey on St Helier's Isle in St Aubin's Bay. The castle buildings were completed shortly before Sir Walter Ralegh was appointed Governor (1600) and called Fort Isabella Bellissima in honour of Queen Elizabeth I. It was considerably reinforced during the Civil War while occupied by Royalists who, after resisting the repeated assaults from Parliamentary forces on the island, surrendered after a 50-day siege. Contemporary documents confirm that the young Prince of Wales stayed here when fleeing from England in 1646, and again three years later when returning to be proclaimed King Charles II. During the Second World War the Germans added to the fortifications by installing a roving searchlight, bunkers and gun batteries. In 1996 Queen Elizabeth II handed the castle, together with Mont Orgueil, to the islanders.

The Guard room displays the various stages in the construction of the castle. The **Militia Museum** contains mementoes of the Royal Jersey Regiment: uniforms, weapons, flags and silver including an unusual snuff-box in the shape of a ram's head.

The Upper Ward encloses the keep, known as the Mount, where the Germans built a concrete fire-control tower surmounted by an anti-aircraft position. There is a fine **view**★ of the castle itself and also of St Aubin's Fort across the bay.

South of the castle a breakwater extends past the chapel on the rock where, according to legend, St Helier lived as a hermit *(procession on or about 16 July, St Helier's Day)*.

■ Excursions Inland
Trinity
From St Helier take A 8 north to Le Mont de la Trinité; at la Rue Asplet turn right onto B 31 towards Trinity Church; this road soon becomes La Rue des Picots passing in front of the zoo (right).

Jersey Zoo★★ – *2-3hr.* The Durrell Wildlife Conservation Trust, with its headquarters at Jersey Zoo (Les Augrès Manor), was founded by the naturalist **Gerald Durrell** in 1963 as a unique centre for research and breeding of rare and endangered species. The high rate of success in this prime objective has led to exchanges with other zoos (Bristol, Newquay, Paignton, Dublin, Washington) and the reintroduction of a number of threatened species into native habitats. The symbol of the Trust is the dodo, the great non-flying bird of Mauritius which was first identified in 1599 and was extinct by 1693.

The undulating park (10 acres) is dedicated to providing compatible environments for some 1 000 animals in cages, temperate housing, landscaped enclosures or open garden and woodland. Exotic species

Asking the way

Jersey has a number of **cycling routes**, marked by blue signs with white writing, and a network of tree-lined lanes, known as **green lanes**, where walkers, cyclists and horse-riders have priority over the car (maximum speed 15mph/24kmph). There are also long stretches of **coastal footpath**. Most of the principal tourist sites are flagged by brown signs with white writing.

When local Jersey people give directions, they tend to refer to the roads by name rather than number; it is therefore well worth obtaining a Perry's Pathfinder map, which marks footpaths, car parks and refreshment facilities, or the Town and Island Map, which contains information on green lanes, coastal footpaths, sites of special interest, heritage sights and Second World War sites; it is produced by Jersey Tourism which also publishes a cycling and walking guide.

© Jersey.com

Orang-utan, Jersey Zoo

the silverback "Jambo" (1961-92); orang-utans from Sumatra and the less extrovert lemurs from Madagascar, marmosets and tamarins from Brazil, some of which roam freely in the thick shrubbery.

Tortoises, terrapins, snakes, frogs, toads and lizards, happy to lounge in their warmed enclosures among sprigs of flowering orchids, thrive in the **Gaherty Reptile Breeding Centre**. A special unit enables visitors to observe the activities of rare fruit bats and the intriguingly named aye-aye by subdued artificial light.

of plants are grown to provide the animals with both food and natural cover – their controlled diets being otherwise supplemented with locally produced organic meat, fruit and vegetables.

Residents include babirusas from Indonesia; spectacled bears from the forest uplands of Bolivia and Peru (the only bear indigenous to South America); snow leopards and cheetahs; a long list of birds includes the St Lucia parrot, the Mexican thick-billed parrot, the white-eared pheasant from China, the pink pigeon from Mauritius, the white-naped crane native of Japan and Korea, the Rothschild mynah bird, the Chilean flamingo and the Waldrapp Ibis.

The most popular animals, however, are probably the primates: a dynasty of lowland gorillas descended from

The **Princess Royal Pavilion** presents the history of the Trust and its work on wildlife and conservation (audio-visual presentation) in association with Preservation Trusts in America and Canada. Besides the scientific research, the residential courses, the valuable hands-on approach of animal workshops for children in Jersey and the overseas training programmes, the visitor cannot fail to be impressed by the informal, happy atmosphere of the place which has been so congenial to the successful breeding of endangered species in captivity.

Eric Young Orchid Foundation* – *Victoria Village, Trinity. 1hr. Signs in Victoria village but the Orchid Foundation is difficult to find.*

A fabulous show of prize plants appealing to both amateur and professional growers of orchids is presented here in a Display House. The mission of the Foundation is to "promote orchid improvement for all" – it therefore collaborates on a conservation and research basis with the Royal Horticultural Society and the Royal Botanic Gardens at Kew, and other passionate growers ever fascinated by variations in colour and form achieved by hybridisation. Displays are regularly re-organised to ensure constant shows of species, the groups arranged to allow close study of their distinctive blooms. The five adjacent growing houses *(open but roped off)* are dedicated to the genera Cymbidium, Paphiopedilium or slipper orchids, Cattleya, Phalaenopsis or moth orchids, Odontoglossum or butterfly orchids (including Miltonias or pansy orchids).

Grouville

From St Helier take either A 6 (La route Bagatelle) or A 7 (St Saviour's Hill) northwest; at Five Oaks take A 7 (Princes Tower Road) to the entrance to La Hougue Bie (left).

La Hougue Bie* – *1hr.* The tiny park, encircled by trees, is dominated by a high circular mound.

Its name may be derived from the Old Norse word *haugr* (meaning barrow) and *bie,* a shorthand for Hambye, a Norman lord who in the Middle Ages came to rid Jersey of a dragon that stalked St Lawrence marsh. During the German occupation, the site was heavily fortified, as it provides an excellent **view** over outlying countryside.

Archeology and Geology Museum – Artefacts displayed were brought to light by local excavations – notably from La Cotte de St Brelade, a sea cave in the Ouaisné headland and the Belle Hougue caves on the north coast: remains of mammoths, polished stone axes, flint tools, stone querns for grinding corn (belonging to Neolithic settlers who were farmers), pottery, ornaments; Bronze Age metal objects found in St Lawrence etc. The geology section presents samples of the various rocks and minerals found on the island: shales (south of island), volcanic lavas (north), pink and grey granites and diorites (northwest and southwest), Rozel conglomerates or puddingstone.

Neolithic Tomb* – The cruciform passage burial chamber, long suspected by archeologists but excavated only in 1924, dates from 3500 BC. Similar tombs have been discovered in England and Brittany. The grave was originally built above ground with upright stones and roofed with granite slabs before being covered by a mound of earth and rubble (40ft/12m). A passage (33ft/10m long) leads to the funeral chamber (10ft/3mx30ft/9m), which is covered with huge capstones (the heaviest weighing 25 tonnes); this central space opens into three smaller chambers. The central granite pillar is a modern addition to support the large capstones which were found to be cracked.

Chapels – The mound is surmounted by two medieval chapels: the **Chapel of Our Lady of the Dawn** (Notre Dame de la Clarté) dates from the 12C; the altar (late Medieval) came from Mont Orgueil Castle. The abutting **Jerusalem Chapel** was built in 1520 by Dean Richard Mabon after a pilgrimage to Jerusalem. The interior bears traces of frescoes of two archangels.

German Occupation Museum – A German bunker, built in 1942 as a communications centre, houses radio equipment, weapons, medals, original documents (orders and propaganda), photographs of the period and a memorial to the slave workers.

Waterworks Valley

From St Helier take the main road A 1 (La Route St Aubin), turn right onto A 10 (Le Mont Felard) and continue through St Lawrence.

La Vallée de St Laurent, set between St Peter's Valley and Waterworks Valley, boasts a number of important traditional Norman-style stone (granite) farmhouses and remnants of water-powered mills. Several of the most typical houses now belong to the National Trust of Jersey, including La Ferme Morel, Le Colombier, and the 17C cottage locally named Le Rât. Of the six mills which operated in the valley, one is in working order although some were reactivated during the occupation; the streams now supply Jersey's mains water supply.

Fork right along La Rue des Corvées which joins C 119 (La Rue de la Patente and Le Chemin des Moulins).

Hamptonne Country Life Museum★ – Hamptonne House was built by Vicomte (Sheriff of the Court) Laurens Hamptonne – the same man who proclaimed Charles II King in the market place in St Helier in February 1649. The land was acquired in 1633, the house is presumed to have been completed in 1637.

Aligned along the northern yard are a series of restored 19C **farm outbuildings**, arranged as a labourer's cottage, coach-house, bake-house, wash-house and stables. A gateway leads to the orchard and open meadow beyond, and to the south-facing walled garden overlooked by the square pigeon-house or colombier (one of two on Jersey).

The **Langlois Building**, on the south side, is an upper hall house of a type found in medieval Brittany, accommodating animals at ground level and human beings above. The interior is thoughtfully recreated to suggest life in the 18C with hand-made country-style oak furniture.

Hamptonne House, partly thatched and partly slate-roofed, is brought to life by museum staff, dressed in period costume, who complete the picture of the family and its way of life during the 17C and early 18C.

The Syvret Building provides space for thematic exhibitions relating to rural practices. The northern section shelters a cider barn complete with apple crusher and twin-screw press (activated in October). Home-made produce including bread baked in cabbage and cider are available from the café.

St Peter's Valley

From St Helier take A 1 (La Route St Aubin); after Millbrook, turn right onto A 11 (Le Chemins des Moulins); when the main road curves sharply to the left, bear right onto B 89 (sign: German Underground Hospital).

German Underground Hospital* – This large complex of tunnels is kept as a compelling memorial to the forced labourers (Spaniards, Moroccans, Alsatian Jews, Poles, Frenchmen, Russians) who worked on its construction for 3.5 years under the severest conditions. Note that some visitors may find the visit rather harrowing, others may suffer from claustrophobia.

Hohlgangsanlagen 8 was intended as a secure, bomb-proof artillery barracks, complete with accommodation and a storage facility for ammunition. In January 1944, still incomplete, it was converted into a hospital equipped with an operating theatre, five 100-bed wards, X-ray room, mortuary, stores, kitchen, staff quarters etc. On entering the long dark galleries hewn deep into the solid rock, the temperature drops, the air is damp, the sound of footsteps is amplified through the concrete emptiness. Wartime films, archive photographs, newspaper cuttings, letters and memorabilia document the personal suffering and trauma of those caught up in the events.

The **Occupation Walk** up onto high ground opposite the complex leads to an area fortified by genuine anti-aircraft gun positions, crawl trenches, barbed wire entanglements and personnel shelters *(leaflet available from Visitor Centre). Return downhill; turn right onto A 11 and continue uphill on La Vallée de St Pierre to Quétivel Mill.*

Moulin de Quétivel – The **mill** (pre-1309), on a bend in St Peter's Valley, is one of several which once operated by the stream until they were made obsolete by steam power. During the German Occupation the machinery was restored for temporary service before being largely destroyed by fire (1969). Since 1979, re-equipped with parts from other disused Jersey mills, Quetivel has been in operation grinding locally-grown grain and producing stone-ground flour for sale.

© Jersey.com

Continue north by A 11; take the second turning right onto C 124 (Rue du Petit Aleval).

Living Legend – Inside the granite buildings unfurls the entertaining multi-sensory experience that relates the history and myths of Jersey. The time-travellers explore a labyrinth of mysterious chambers, make their way through castle towers and across the decks of a Victorian paddle-steamer to discover the lives of past islanders and stories told of heroes and villains. Atmosphere is enhanced by visual and sound effects (holograms, lasers, wind machines...).

From the mill pond the water is channelled by the mill leat down through the wood (inhabited by red squirrels and woodpeckers) to the mill wheel, a pitch-back overshot wheel. The tour shows each stage of the process from the arrival of the grain by hoist in the loft to the production of stone-ground flour for sale on the ground floor. Most of the grinding stones are made of French burr, quarried near Orly Airport south of Paris; these are composed of segments set with plaster of Paris and last a hundred years. A pair of stones will produce 25 tons of flour before needing to be dressed, when the grooves are recut to the required depth using a tool called a "bill" – this process can take a miller about a week.

St Peter's Village

From St Helier take A 1 (La Route St Aubin) west; after passing through Millbrook and Beaumont, turn right onto A 12 (Le Beau Mont) to St Peter's Village.

St Peter's Church – The Parish church has a remarkable steeple (124ft high) which by chance escaped from being faced with cement; at its apex is a red navigation light used by aircraft coming in to land at the airport nearby. Behind the altar is a reredos by George Tinworth, commissioned in the 1880s from Royal Doulton.

Jersey Motor Museum – This collection of veteran and vintage vehicles, all in working order and appearing at rallies in Jersey and elsewhere, includes the 1936 Rolls-Royce Phantom III, used by General Montgomery in 1944 during D-Day preparations, and the 1964 Hillman Husky which belonged to Sir Winston Churchill. Cars by Ford, Austin, Talbot, Triumph, Bentley and Jaguar contrast with Allied and German military vehicles, bicycles (c 1869 Boneshaker) and motorbikes. Other items include several period brass lamps, classic pedal- and petrol-driven children's cars, toys, an old AA callbox and a car from the Jersey steam railway.

On the opposite side of the square is an underground bunker built by the German Organization Todt in 1942, strategically placed so as to keep surveillance over the airport and access roads to the west of the island.

■ Tour of Island

① From St Helier to Corbière 10mi/18km – about 2hr

From St Helier take A 1 (La Route de St Aubin) west.

Millbrook – The Villa Millbrook was once home to Sir Jesse Boot, the first Baron Trent of Nottingham and founder of Boots the Chemists, who is buried at St Brelade.

St Matthew's Church – The **Glass Church**, as it is also known, was unexceptional until 1934 when **René Lalique** (1860-1945), the French specialist in moulded glass, was invited by Lord Trent's widow to redecorate the interior with dis-

tinctive **glasswork***: the entrance doors are made of panels presenting a row of four angels guarding another behind the main altar. The other decorative element is the flowering lily which appears in the windows, screens and in the Lady Chapel. The luminescent, ethereal quality is most apparent at dusk when the lights are switched on.

Follow the main road (La Route de La Haule) and then A 1 (La Neuve Route).

St Aubin – The little town, which faces east across St Aubin's Bay, is particularly picturesque with its long sandy beach, fishermen's cottages and tall granite merchants' houses lining steep, narrow streets or clinging to the cliffs along the shore. The name is auspicious as St Aubin, besides being Bishop of Angers (d AD 550) during the lifetime of St Helier, was invoked as protector against pirates.

The local church (1892) has a fine stained-glass window made by William Morris & Co.

St Aubin's Fort on the island (*access at low tide*) was built in the reign of Henry VIII to protect the town which enjoyed considerable prosperity during the 17C.

The Corbière Walk from St Helier to Corbière follows the line of the old **Jersey Railway** which opened in 1870 and ran from St Helier to St Aubin before being extended.

Turn left off the main road onto B 57 (La Route de Noirmont) for access to the promontory and Portelet Bay.

Noirmont Point★ – The local saying warns of the onset of gales from the southwest:

"Quand Nièrmont met san bonnet,
Ch'est signe de plyie."
("When Noirmont [Black Hill]
dons his cap,
It is a sign of rain.")

Beyond the pebble beach nestling in **Belcroute** stretches the headland, still scarred by the remains of substantial German fortifications (1941 and 1943-44) including the **Command Bunker** – a post for the naval coastal artillery battery. The most advanced bastion gives fine views of the rocks immediately below and round westwards to the Ile au Guerdain, surmounted by a defensive tower, in the centre of Portelet Bay.

The southernmost parts of the promontory have revealed an important Bronze Age burial ground, not far from the site of the famous cave of La Cotte de St Brelade.

Return to the main road A 13 (La Route des Genets) and then fork left down B 66 (Le Mont Sohier).

St Brelade – This favourite seaside resort is situated in a sheltered bay; its sandy beaches and usually safe waters *(certain areas can be tricky)* are ideal for swimming and water-skiing. A waterfall tumbles over the rocks on the wooded slopes of the **Winston Churchill Memorial Park** which backs the bay.

At the western end of the beach, behind a screen of trees, the parish church and detached medieval chapel are surrounded by a graveyard. At one time this was the resting place of 337 German servicemen who were on the islands as prisoners during the First World War or on active duty during the Occupation: they were re-interred in 1961 at Mont de Huisnes at St Malo.

Parish Church – *Light switch inside on the left of entrance.* The cherished

Church of St Brelade is built of granite from the cliffs of La Moye (meaning rocky headland). The earliest parts of the structure – the chancel, nave and belfry – date from the 11C. In the 12C the church became cruciform with the addition of a transept; the aisles were added later.

The altar is a solid slab of stone, marked with five crosses representing the five wounds of the Crucifixion. The 15C font is made of granite from the Chausey Islands, which lie south of Jersey and belong to France.

Fishermen's Chapel – *Light switch inside on the left of entrance.* The family chapel, which is built of the same granite as the church, is decorated in the interior with delicate medieval **frescoes***. At the east end is an *Annunciation* – dated as c 1375 from the medieval attire of the donors at prayer; the other paintings are from a second phase of work c 1425: the south wall (right of the altar) shows *Adam and Eve* followed by *The Annunciation* and *The Adoration of the Magi,* the west wall bears *The Last Judgement,* on the north wall fragments have been deciphered as *Scenes from the Passion.* The survival of the paintings is largely due to the fact that from c 1550 to the mid 19C the chapel was used as an armoury, housing the parochial cannon, and as a carpenter's shop. The windows, by a local craftsman HT Bosdet (1857-1934), narrate the story of St Brendan, who set sail from the west coast of Ireland in the 6C and is thought to have reached the American continent.

Behind the chapel a short flight of steps leads to a path through the churchyard to the beach; this is the only surviving example of a *perquage*: once commonplace in medieval Europe, these paths were intended as escape routes from a chapel or church traditionally a

St Brelade's Bay

place of sanctuary to the shore and away out to sea.

Continue along the road back into town; turn left onto A 13 (La Route Orange); bear left down B 83 (La Route du Sud) to Corbière.

Corbière – All that remains of the terminus of the Jersey Railway is the concrete platform. As the road descends, a magnificent view is steadily revealed of the rock-strewn point and the white lighthouse rising from its islet: a good place to watch the sun set over the Atlantic. Before the lighthouse *(access on foot at low tide but closed to the public)* was built in 1874, this was a perilous stretch of water where a number of ships foundered, lost to the tide; in clear weather the electric beam carries 17 miles.

2 **From Corbière to Petit Etacquerel**

8mi/13km – 1hr

Follow the road round to the junction with B 35 (La Rue de Sergente); turn left towards the coast.

St Ouen's Bay – The major part of this coastline is taken up with this magnificent, open stretch of sand (5mi) backed by sand dunes. The deep surf which rolls into the bay makes it a favourite spot for experienced surfboard and wind-surf enthusiasts. The firm sand attracts motor and motorcycle racing fans.

In the middle of the bay sits **La Rocco Tower**, the last round tower to be built in Jersey (1800); having been severely damaged during the war, the tower was finally restored during the 1970s.

© Jersey.com

Corbière

Beyond the beach, the landscape is wild and uncultivated, the vegetation sparse. **La Pulente** used to be the main centre for gathering seaweed *(vraic)* which was traditionally used as fertiliser. La Sergenté, also known as the Beehive Hut, is another important Neolithic tomb near to which a large hoard of coins from Brittany was found. The **St Ouen Pond** on the right of the road is also known as La Mare du Seigneur as it once belonged to the Seigneur of St Ouen (the most senior of the island seigneurs resident in St Ouen's Manor). This stretch of fresh water is a haven for birds and wild flowers, notably the Jersey or lax-flowered orchid. The three upright stones Les Trois Rocques are presumed to be part of a dolmen.

Kempt Tower – This defensive tower has been converted into an Interpretation Centre with video theatre, leaflets, maps, photographs and pamphlets about the region: geological features, archeological remains, flora and fauna. The area around it has been made into a nature reserve called **Les Mielles** (the Jersey dialect word for sand dunes) to monitor and protect indigenous plants, birds and butterflies.

Follow B 35 (La Route des Laveurs); turn left onto C 114 (Le Mont des Corvées).

Battle of Flowers Museum – The **Battle of Flowers**, held on the second Thursday in August along Victoria Avenue in St Helier, was started in 1902 to celebrate the coronation of Edward VII. Traditionally, the floats were broken up after the parade and the crowd pelted one another with the flowers, then mostly hydrangeas. Today, a collection of floats which over the years have been entered in the wild flower category, is here presented by their creator. The tableaux are made up of different grasses and concentrate on animal subjects.

Return to the coastal road; bear right onto B 35 (La Route de l'Étacq).

Petit Etacquerel – A defensive tower guards the point which marks the northern end of St Ouen's Bay. It is here that in 1651 Admiral Blake landed with the Parliamentary forces which forced the Royalists to surrender.

③ From Grosnez Point to Rozel Bay *17mi/28km – 2.5hr*

The northern coast of the island is less densely populated than other parts as steep rocky cliffs alternate with small sandy bays. Cliff paths, which stretch from Plémont Bay to Sorel Point and beyond, provide spectacular views of the uneven coastline and the open sea

---

Birds to be seen around Les Mielles

Besides such common birds as blackbirds, thrushes, wrens, robins and tits, the sand dunes harbour colonies of kestrels and skylarks and attract such migrants as willow warblers, stonechats and wheatears. Stretches of fresh open water and reed-beds provide popular habitats for moorhens, coots, ducks (mallard, tufted, shoveler), kingfishers, sandpipers, lapwings, herons and snipe. Please show consideration by not disturbing pairs or fledgelings through the nesting and breeding season (April to July).

During the summer, the coastal footpath from Plemont to Grève de Lecq affords good sightings of sea-birds: fulmars (May to September), puffins and razorbills – notably early morning and early evening. In winter, Brent geese, plovers, redshanks, turnstones, dunlin, bar-tailed godwits, curlews, oystercatchers, teal, snipe, lapwings and herons may be seen feeding on an incoming tide.

to France, Guernsey and Alderney (although they say that a clear view of Alderney heralds rain). Early-crop potatoes are grown on the steeply sloping hillsides (côtils).

Continue north by bearing left onto B 55 (La Route du Ouest): bear left again to reach the car park and look-out point at Grosnez.

Grosnez Point* – An area of desolate heathland, covered with gorse and heather and known as Les Landes, extends from Etacquerel to Grosnez Point. South-west of the racecourse sits **Le Pinacle**, a strange yet impressive rock that has been found to be associated with pagan rituals since Neolithic, Bronze Age, Iron Age, even Roman times.

Dramatically positioned overlooking the sea are the ruins of a medieval stronghold which must have provided a place of temporary refuge against invasion. Little remains of **Grosnez Castle** (c 1373-1540) besides the curtain wall with ditch, gateway and drawbridge; however it enjoys magnificent views out to sea, of Sark and the other islands (northwest).

Return to B 55; in Portinfer turn left onto C 105 (La Route de Plémont); fork left to Grève au Lançon; eventually the road skirts the holiday village to end in a car park from where a footpath runs along the coast to Grève de Lecq.

Steep cliffs containing caves shelter this attractive small bay, **Grève au Lanchon**, which has a sandy beach at low tide. The rocky promontory **Plémont Point** projects into the sea giving a fine view of the cliffs.

Return along C 105 (La Route de Plémont); turn left onto B 55 (La Route de Vinchelez) from Grosnez, which leads to Leoville in the parish of St Mary. Turn left onto B 65 (Le Mont de la Grève de Lecque).

Grève de Lecq – This charming sandy bay with its stream and mill was defended against invasion most recently by the Germans, in the Second World War, and earlier against the French in the 18C-19C. The defensive tower was built in 1780 although the conical hill behind is from an Iron Age fortification.

The **barracks** were built between 1810 and 1815 to accommodate the 150 British soldiers who manned the gun batteries on the slopes around the bay – although blocks were built at Bonne Nuit Bay, Rozel Bay and St Peter's Parish, these here are the only ones to survive. There were two blocks, each consisting of four rooms for the soldiers and two for the NCOs; the central building was for the officers. Behind stood the ablutions block and two prison cells; to the south was the stabling. In spring and early summer the area is abloom with wild flowers: gorse, daffodils, bluebells, foxgloves.

The water's edge is broken by jagged rocks locally known as

Paternoster Rocks after the many prayers uttered through time by passing fishermen, remembering colleagues who perished there. Far out to sea is the French coast.

From Grève de Lecq continue along the road B 40 (La Mont de Ste Marie); turn left onto B 33 (La Verte Rue) and left again before the West View Hotel onto C 103.

La Mare Vineyards – The estate of an 18C farmhouse has been planted with the only vineyards and cider orchard in Jersey. An introductory video film, describing its history, the vineyards, the har-

Bouley Bay

vest and the wine-making process, adds to the interest of touring the vineyards and the gleaming modern vintry, where German-style white wines are produced and may be tasted: Clos de la Mare, Clos de Seyval and Blayney Special Reserve.

Minor roads run east to St John's Parish and north to the coast.

Sorel Point – The section of road named **La Route du Nord** is dedicated to the islanders who suffered during the German Occupation (stone in car park). It runs from Sorel Point where a

© Jersey.com

mysterious pool (24ft wide by 15ft deep) is revealed in the rocks at low tide: disputes continue as to whether it is a natural or man-made phenomenon; the pool is known as the Fairies' Bath (Lavoir des Dames). To the east is Ronez Point, a headland scarred by granite quarries.

Drive through St John; turn left onto A 9 (La Route des Issues); after the Jersey Pearl Centre fork left again onto B 67 (La Route de Mont Mado). Turn left onto C 99, a minor road to Bonne Nuit Bay and Giffard Bay.

Bonne Nuit Bay – This bay, which may well have been haunted by smugglers and pirates in the past, is a favourite place for swimming

Continue along C 103 to the Priory Inn.

Devil's Hole* – *Park by the inn and take the concrete path down to the cliff.* The blow hole is an impressive sight dramatised by the amplified thunder of the sea entering the cave below. The name is thought to derive from the old French Creux de Vis meaning screwhole, although other stories tell of the wreck of a French ship in 1871, whose figurehead resembled a devil.

and sailing. Charles II is supposed to have returned from exile to England from this attractive bay where a stone jetty shelters the tiny harbour. The fort, La Crête, at the east end was built in 1835.

From here a footpath follows the coast to Bouley Bay; to reach Bouley Bay by car, take C 98, B 63, C 97 (Rue des Platons).

Bouley Bay – In the 19C it was proposed that the deep sandy bay protected by a jetty and backed by high granite cliffs should be transformed into a sheltered harbour. Today it is a safe, popular place for swimming.

Return towards Trinity; turn left onto B 31 (La Rue ès Picots) past Jersey Zoo before turning sharp left onto C 93 (La Rue du Rocquier) to Rozel Bay.

Rozel Bay – Part of the bay is taken up with a fishing port where the boats go aground at low tide. Above the bay, at the northern end, traces of a great earth rampart survive from the Castel de Rozel, an Iron Age settlement. Many coins from different eras have also been recovered from the area. At the opposite end, sits **Le Couperon**, a Neolithic passage grave (2500 BC). Below it, at the water's edge among the rocks at low tide, are a profusion of pools inhabited by small crustacea making it a wonderful place for amateur zoologists and children to explore.

4️⃣ **From Rozel Bay to St Helier** *13mi – 90min*

The road turns inland before returning to the coast above Fliquet Bay and finally meandering down to the water line: a submarine cable runs from the Martello Tower to France.

Fliquet Bay is a rocky bay between La Coupe and Verclut Points: an ideal place for deciphering the volcanic evolution of the island.

Either follow the road to St Martin or make a detour to explore the country roads – B 38 (La Grande Route de Rozel), B 91 (La Rue des Pelles), B 91 (La Route du Villot), B 29 (Le Mont des Ormes) to Verclut Point (left) and to Gorey Harbour (right).

St Catherine's Bay★ – The long breakwater (0.5mi), which protects the bay to the north, was part of a British government scheme (1847-55) to create a huge naval "harbour of refuge" as the French developed coastal stations around Cherbourg: work to build a second breakwater was abandoned in 1852 as relations with Napoleon III improved. From the lighthouse at the end there is a magnificent **view★★** of sandy bays alternating with rocky promontories along the coast southwards. Out to sea lie the Ecréhou islets administered by St Martin's Parish – once a favoured trading bank for smugglers and now a popular spot for a Sunday picnic.

Faldouet Dolmen – *Bear right off the coast road (La Route d'Anne Port).* A tree-lined path leads to this dolmen, which is 49ft long and dates from 2500 BC. The funeral chamber (20ft wide) is covered by a block of granite weighing 25 tonnes. Excavation has revealed a number of vases, stone pendants and polished stone axes.

Gorey – This charming little port at the northern end of Grouville Bay is dominated by the proud walls of Mont Orgueil Castle set on its rocky promontory. Attractive old houses line the quay where yachts add colour to the scene in

summer. In the days of the Jersey Eastern Railway (1873-1929) there was a steamship service from Gorey to Normandy.

Mont Orgueil Castle* – *45min.* Gorey Castle received its present name in 1468 from Henry V's brother, Thomas, Duke of Clarence, who was so impressed by the castle's position and its defensive strength that he called it Mount Pride (Mont Orgueil in French). Over the centuries the castle has served as a residence to the Lords and Governors of the island, including Sir Walter Ralegh (1600-03), a prison for English political prisoners, and a refuge for a spy-network during the French Revolution. The earliest buildings date back to the 13C when King John lost control of Normandy and built a castle to defend the island from invasion; new fortifications were added over

© Jersey.com

the years as assaults from bows and arrows evolved into mortar attack and cannon fire. It was subsequently used as a prison and eventually ceded by the Crown to the States of Jersey in 1907; in 1996 Queen Elizabeth II handed the castle to the islanders.

The castle is built on a concentric plan, each system of defence being independent of the other. The solid walls founded on the granite rocks are a formidable obstacle. It is like threading a maze to walk up the complex network of passages and steps to the summit. The **view**** from the top is extensive: down into Port Gorey, south over the broad sweep of Grouville Bay, north to the rocks of Petit Portelet and west to the French coast.

A series of waxwork tableaux in the rooms of the castle illustrates significant events in the history of Mont Orgueil including one of Charles II during his exile in Jersey as the guest of the Governor George de Carteret, to whom he granted the land in Virginia that became New Jersey.

Take the A 3 (Gorey Coast Road) along the waterfront.

Royal Bay of Grouville – The Parish of Grouville is graced with Jersey's finest bay, a magnificent crescent of sand stretching from Gorey harbour to La Rocque Point. The skyline is punctuated by a series of Martello towers and forts which were constructed during the Napoleonic Wars: of these the Seymour and Icho towers (1811) may be reached on foot at low tide.

Jersey Pottery – *45min.* A paved garden, hung with baskets of flowers and refreshed by fountains, surrounds the workshops where the distinctive pottery is produced. Each stage in the process is explained on large panels and the visitor can watch the craftsmen at work at their various skills or browse in the museum. The show room displays the full range of products for sale.

Royal Jersey Golf Club – The local golf course enjoys a particularly picturesque position; founded in 1878, it was granted its Royal Charter by Queen Victoria.

Grouville Church – Originally dedicated to St Martin of Tours, the church has an unusual 15C granite font and a number of early examples of locally-made church plate.

St Clement's – St Clement is Jersey's smallest parish, named after the church dedicated to Clement I, the third Pope (AD 68-78); it was here that Hugo wrote two volumes of poetry: *Les Chatiments* and *Les Contemplations,* before departing to Guernsey...

The dolmen at Mont Ubé, the 11ft menhir known as **La Dame Blanche**, and a tall granite outcrop called Rocqueberg suggest that this section of the island was well inhabited by Neolithic man. The earliest priory on the site belonged to the Abbey of Mont St Michel.

The oldest extant parts of the present church date from the 12C; the wall paintings from the 15C (*St Michael slaying the Dragon; the legend of the* Three Living and Three Dead Kings).

St Clement's Bay – This sandy bay stretches from Plat Rocqe Point, past Le Hocq Point, marked by a defensive tower, to Le Nez Point (*2mi*). Out to sea strong tides sweep through, continually churning the water. In 1781 Baron de Rullecourt landed with 600 French troops at the eastern end of the bay in the last French attempt to capture Jersey.

From A 4 (La Grande Route de St Clement) turn onto B 48 (La Rue du Pontille), which leads into A 5 (St Clement's Road), to reach Samarès Manor (right).

Samarès Manor – The name Samarès is probably derived from the Norman *salse marais,* the salt-pans which provided the lord of the manor with a significant part of his revenue. The history of the estate began in the 11C when William Rufus granted the Samarès fief to his faithful servant Rodolph of St Hilaire. In the 17C Philippe Dumaresq decided to give the estate a new look; he drained the marsh by building a canal to St Helier and imported trees and vines from France. The gardens were landscaped and largely re-planted by Sir James Knott who acquired the property in 1924; the herb garden is later still. Of particular interest in the grounds is the rare 11C dovecot; in the house there is the Norman undercroft or manor chapel crypt and the walnut-panelled dining room.

Continue west on A 4 (the coast road) to Dicq Corner; see plan of St Helier.

Le Rocher des Proscrits (Z) – *Small plaque facing the road.* On the east side of the White Horse Inn, a slipway descends to the beach and a group of rocks, Le Rocher des Proscrits (The Rock of the Exiles), where **Victor Hugo** (*see p 62*) used to meet regularly with fellow exiles. ■

GUERNSEY*

Guernsey is the second largest of the Channel Islands (24sq mi/ 63km²): less sophisticated than its larger neighbour, it has its own particular charm: a slower tempo, the Regency elegance of the capital St Peter Port, the proximity of other islands – Sark, Herm and Jethou. Since the Second World War its main sources of income have been tourism, offshore finance and insurance, and tomatoes.

Population 58 867
Michelin Atlas p 5 or Map 503

Guernsey is shaped like a right-angled triangle; the west coast forms the hypotenuse, the south coast the base and the east coast the perpendicular. From the air the whole island seems to be covered with small fields and dwellings, and many glasshouses, linked by a network of narrow lanes. There is little open country – L'Andresse

Common at the north end and a narrow strip of wild country along the southern cliffs where flowers abound in spring. The **water lane**, where a stream runs in a channel down the side of the road, is a special feature of Guernsey, as through Moulin Huet Valley, Petit Bot Valley.

Economy – As the island slopes from south to north away from the sun, most of the crops are grown under glass. The most famous export, the Guernsey tomato, was first grown in 1893 among the grapes in the greenhouses, hence the name vinery for a tomato farm. Grapes are still grown as well as melons, peas, potatoes and, of course, flowers. Fishing is still an important activity to supply the tables of the inhabitants and the visitors.

The abundant and varied supply of **local granite**, particularly from the Clos du Valle, has provided the islanders with an excellent and attractive building stone, although it is hard to shape or carve: pink or brownish-red from Côbo and Albecq, golden-yellow from L'Ancresse and grey, blue and black from other northern quarries.

Historical notes – Like its neighbours, Guernsey was inhabited in prehistoric times and is rich in

Practical Information

Tourist Information Centre – www.guernseytouristboard.com
PO Box 23, White Rock, St Peter Port, Guernsey GY1 3AN
☎ 01481 723 552, 723 555 (accommodation); Fax 01481 714 951;
enquiries@tourism.guernseytouristboard.com

Guernsey Airport, La Villiaze, Forest, Guernsey ☎ 01481 237 267;
Fax 01481 234 329

Emergencies – Dial 112 or 999 and ask for required service: fire, ambulance, police.

Access – By air or sea from the mainland or from Alderney or Jersey. From St Peter Port there are regular services by sea to Sark and Herm.

Guernsey Airport – ☎ 01481 23 77 66.

Motoring – Hire cars are available but visitors may bring their own vehicles. **Petrol stations** are closed on Sundays. **Parking** in Guernsey is free but controlled; from Monday to Saturday until 6pm vehicles should display a **parking clock** (provided in hire cars or available from newsagents and the Visitor Information Centre).

Highway Code – **Seat-belts** must be worn at all times. **Children** under the age of 14 must travel in the rear of the car.

A **yellow line** painted across the road at a junction serves as a STOP or HALT sign and requires drivers to stop before emerging onto the major road.

A **yellow grid** at an intersection requires drivers not to enter the box unless their way ahead is clear.

Filter and Turn at roundabouts requires drivers to give way to the first car from the right before entering onto the roundabout themselves.

The **speed limit** is 25mph in built-up areas and 35mph elsewhere.

Accidents involving injury or dispute about who was at fault must be reported to a policeman (in uniform or honorary: ask a local person) and the vehicles should not be moved from the scene before the incident has been reported. In other cases the parties should reach agreement and exchange details.

Cycling – The 11 main designated cycle routes are marked with round coloured symbols. Bicycles can be hired in St Peter Port, St Sampson and St Martin's and from other companies which offer free delivery and collection.

Guided tours – Various tours of the coast, the centre of the island and heritage properties are organised by Guernseybus, Piquet House, opposite the Town Church.

Information about which **fortifications** have been restored as much as possible to their former condition is printed in the leaflet *Fortress Guernsey*, available from tourist information centres.

Floral Displays – Wild flowers are particularly colourful from April to June. In May and June there are guided walks of the **orchid fields** owned by La Societé Guernesiaise near the west coast. The **Floral Guernsey Show** takes place during the first week in June in Cambridge Park in St Peter Port.

Shopping – The shops of St Peter Port offer a wide range of fashion at prices which do not include VAT. Among the craft outlets are jewellery, knitwear, pottery, clockmaking, copperware, woodcarving. It is also possible to send flowers by post (☎ 01481 248 185 Guernsey Freesia Centre, Route Carre, St Sampson's; ☎ 08702 421 010; Fax 01481 255 590 Guernsey Fresh Flowers, La Couture Road, St Peter Port).

Licensed Premises – Bars are open from 10.30am to 11.45pm. On Sundays bars holding a family permit open from 12 noon to 3.30pm; they may also serve alcohol from 6pm to 12.45am but only as an accompaniment to food.

Entertainment – Cinema, theatre and a concert hall at the Beau Séjour Leisure Centre.

Sport and Leisure – The sandy beaches and rocky promontories are excellent for bathing, surfing and exploring rock pools; *east coast* – Fermain Bay, *south coast* – Petit Bot Bay, L'Erée Bay, *west coast* - Cobo Bay, Port Soif Bay, Portelet Bay, Bazon Bay, *north coast* - L'Ancresse Bay. There is a clifftop footpath along the south coast (16mi/25km) and inland paths shown on the *Not for Motorists Map.*

There are facilities for sailing, windsurfing, cycling, canoeing, fishing, lawn bowls, golf, horse riding.

The **Beau Séjour Leisure Centre** offers various sports and leisure facilities – tennis, crazy golf, keep-fit, weight training, badminton, table tennis, squash, team sports, ten pin bowling, roller skating, two swimming pools, a leisure pool and learner pool, water slides, sauna, steam room and a solarium.

Bronze and Iron Age monuments such as dolmens. Traces of the Romans' presence consist of a Roman vessel and amphora raised from the sea off St Peter Port and other articles found in excavations in the town.

Christianity may have come in the 6C with St Sampson who arrived from South Wales with his nephew St Magloire, although there are indications that the 10 island parishes may have been established earlier, based on agricultural units. In 933 Guernsey was annexed by the Duke of Normandy and after 1066 was attached to the English Crown; all the charters granted to the island since 1394 are housed in the Greffe in the Royal Court

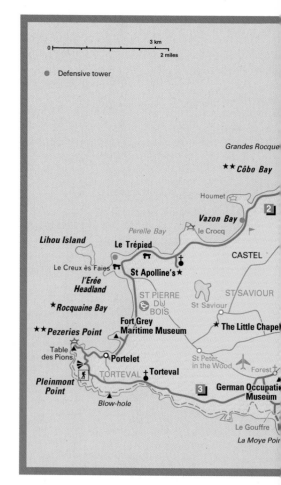

House in St Peter Port. Despite the loss of Normandy to the French in 1204, the link with the Crown was not severed until the Civil War when Guernseymen, angered by the exacting behaviour of the previous English Governor, declared their loyalty to Parliament, although under the Constitution they had no right to do so.

At the Restoration a petition was presented to Charles II humbly begging a royal pardon, which was granted.

Although the Channel Islanders are not obliged to fight except to defend their islands and the monarch, many have served with the British forces: the Royal Guernsey Light Infantry suffered heavy

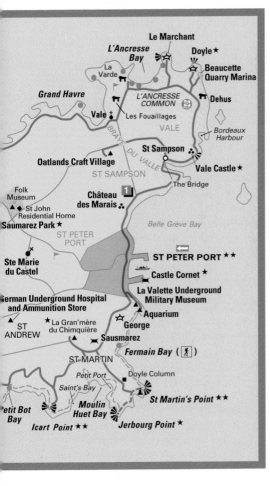

casualties at Cambrai in 1917. Since 1939 201 Squadron of the RAF has been affiliated to the island, confirming the link established in the 1920s when it operated flying boats from Calshot.

Second World War – On 30 June 1940 German aircraft executed a raid on St Peter Port. The following day a German plane landed at the airport, its passengers charged with taking possession of the island. For Hitler this was to be the first step to invading mainland Britain. Over the ensuing five years, Guernsey became one of the most heavily fortified outposts of occupied Europe: many scars were left by the compact reinforced concrete fortifications that made up the Atlantic Wall, although not all are accessible to the public (the

Famous Guernseymen

Despite its size, Guernsey has nurtured several famous men: two Lord Mayors of London – Paul Le Mesurier (1793-94) and Peter Perchard of Hatton Garden (1804-05); Admiral Lord James de Saumarez (1757-1836) who fought against the French in the Napoleonic Wars; Major-General Sir Isaac Brock (1769-1812) who fought under Nelson and died in the defence of Canada against the Americans at Queenstown Heights; Thomas de la Rue (1773-1866) who made his fortune in London printing playing cards, postage stamps and currency notes.

Famous residents include **Victor Hugo** (1802-85) who lived in St Peter Port from 1855-70 while working on several of his most important writings: *Les miserables; Les contemplations (Contemplations); La légende des siècles (The Legend of the Centuries), Les chansons des rues et des bois (The Songs of the Streets and the Woods) and Les travailleurs de la mer (The Toilers of the Sea)*. This latter work is set in Guernsey and carries the dedication: "I dedicate this book to the rock of hospitality, to this corner of old Norman land where resides the noble little people of the sea, to the island of Guernsey, severe and yet gentle..." It was on Guernsey that François Truffaut filmed a number of sequences for his film *Adèle H* about the daughter of Victor Hugo.

As an official of the UK postal services, Anthony Trollope recommended a system of pillar boxes – one of which is still in use.

headquarters of the Luftwaffe are located in the garden of a private house). Guernsey was finally liberated on 9 May 1945.

Constitution – The Bailiwick of Guernsey comprises the islands of Guernsey, Alderney, Sark, Herm and Jethou. The local parliament, known as the States of Deliberation, consists of 45 deputies elected by public suffrage for three years, 10 Douzeniers nominated by the Parish Councils for one year, the Attorney-General and the Solicitor-General. It is presided over by the Bailiff who is also president of the Royal Court which consists of 12 Jurats, appointed by the States of Election, and the Crown Officers. Proceedings are in English although French is still used for the formalities.

■ St Peter Port★★

The island capital is built on a most attractive site on a hillside on the east coast overlooking a safe anchorage protected from high seas by Herm and Sark. The medieval town by the shore was rebuilt after bombardment during the Civil War. Another building boom, financed by the profits earned from privateering in the late 18C, produced a delightful Regency town built in a variety of local granite embellished by elegant garden railings. Guernsey's popularity as a tourist destination in the Victorian era was assured by a visit made by Queen Victoria in 1846, commemorated two years later by the 100ft Victoria Tower designed by William Collings.

Castle Cornet (Z)★ – *2hr.* The castle suffered its greatest misfortune not in war but in a storm in 1672 when a lightning strike ignited the

Castle Cornet

© Gemsey.com

gunpowder store in the old tower keep. The explosion decapitated the castle, destroying not only the tower but the medieval banqueting hall and the Governor's house, and killed his wife and daughter.

History – The original castle (c 1206) was reinforced under Elizabeth I and again under Victoria. The **Prisoners' Walk** is the original barbican – an unusual and most effective piece of defence work. The castle was occupied by the French from 1338 to 1343 and attacked on various occasions including in 1356, 1372 and 1380 (during the Hundred Years War after Edward III had ordered that the town's defences be improved). The fortress was further reinforced in the 16C while the French occupied Sark (1549-53). During the Civil War the islanders sided with Parliament but the castle remained loyal to the king, the last of the royalist strongholds to surrender (1651) after holding out for eight years; many of the 10 000 cannon-balls fired into St Peter Port were retrieved by young boys who sold them back to the castle. The hospital and married quarters were added between 1745 and 1750 to improve living conditions for garrison forces engaged in the French wars.

The castle was superseded as principal defensive stronghold when Fort George was built shortly after the outbreak of the French Revolution. During the 20C, the citadel was fitted with two 12-pounder quick-firing guns and equipped with searchlights: these were fitted so as to monitor defences at water-level. The Germans further installed a series of concrete shelters and anti-aircraft emplacements. An exhibition in the Main Guard graphically relates the **Story of Castle Cornet** from prehistoric to present times.

In the guardroom at the entrance of the castle, built in Victorian times, is a display relating to the history of **201 Guernsey's Own Squadron**.

On the Saluting Platform in the outer bailey the ceremony of the **noonday gun** is performed by two men dressed in the Guernsey Militia uniform; one trains a telescope on the town clock and the other fires the cannon (beware of the extremely loud bang!).

From the Citadel there is a fine **view*** of the harbour and town *(west)*, St Sampson, Vale Castle and Alderney *(22mi north)*, Herm, Sark and the French coast *(east)* and Jersey *(south)*.

Gardens – Based on historic records, efforts have been made to recreate gardens from the 16C (Sutler's Garden outside the resident keeper's house), 17C (Lambert Garden created by Sir John Lambert, "The Knight of the Golden Tulip", one of Cromwell's favourites, who won acclaim growing tulips in

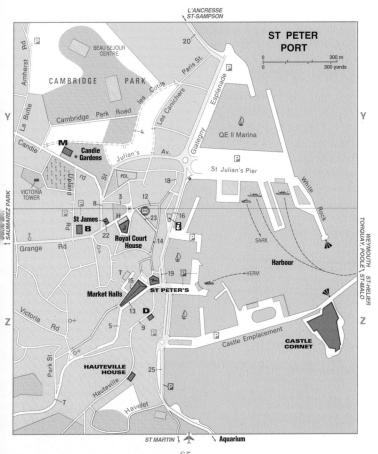

Wimbledon) and 18C (Governor's Garden and Master Gunner's Garden as laid out in 1735).

Museums – The **Maritime Museum** relates the island's maritime history from the Gallo-Roman period to the present day. Exhibitions centre on the harbour, Roman and medieval trade, fish and fishing, smuggling, privateering, the Royal Navy; there is a gallery of marine art, a carpenter's workshop, displays on shipbuilding and cross-Channel steamers, divers and lifeboats. A **Militia Museum**, housed in the Hospital Building (1746), contains two collections: the Spencer Collection *(lower floor)* of uniforms and insignia of the Channel Islands militias, and on the upper floor, regimental silver, musical instruments and mementoes of the Royal Guernsey Militia which was disbanded in 1939. Collections of weapons used by the militia and other regiments connected with Guernsey; Civil War armaments are housed in the **Armoury**.

Harbour (YZ) – The large modern harbour is a scene of constant activity bustling with car and passenger ferries to the mainland and neighbouring islands, fishing boats and private yachts. The north pier was added in the 18C to the original 13C pier to form the Old Harbour. The Castle Pier and St Julian's Pier out to White Rock were built between 1835 and 1909; the Jetty was added in the 1920s. The North Marina provides more accommodation for private craft.

It is worth strolling out to White Rock or visiting the Castle for a fine **view** of the town, the harbour and the neighbouring islands.

St Peter's★ – The Town Church, as it is known, was begun by William the Conqueror in 1048, and completed around 1475. The nave and west door are part of the original Norman structure. In those days it doubled as a fort and in the past it has housed the guns of the

Victoria Marina

© Gemsey.com

artillery, the fire engine, and the flower market on wet days. The interior is furnished with an interesting range of stained glass and a handsome collection of memorials and monuments commemorating famous Guernseymen.

Market Halls (Z) – On the right is the first covered market to be built comprising Les Halles with the Assembly Rooms above, completed in 1782. Opposite is the single-storey Doric-style meat market (1822). "Les Arcades, 1830" *(on the left)* is very handsome despite the loss of the final bay. The Fish Market, with its row of round windows like great port-holes was finished in 1877. Finally, the Vegetable Market was constructed in 1879. All stand on the site of the Rectory Garden.

26 Cornet Street (ZD) – This Victorian shop, complete with period reeded shutters in the bay windows, carefully recreates a sweet-shop and parlour as it would have been in 1900. It also serves as the headquarters of the National Trust for Guernsey.

Continue up Cornet Street some distance (numbering system is deceptive).

Hauteville House (Z)★ – *38 Hauteville.* **Victor Hugo** was exiled from his native France for political reasons in 1851. After a year in Brussels and three in Jersey, from which he was expelled because a fellow exile made disparaging remarks about Queen Victoria, he came to Guernsey. He bought this great white house – supposedly haunted – in 1856 for a derisory sum.

Set back from the street, the plain façade gives no hint of the incongruous and eccentric decor inside. During his 14 years' residence Hugo re-decorated the interior, doing much of the work himself: every inch of wall and ceiling is covered with wood carvings or tiles (from Delft or Rouen), tapestries or silk fabric. In the dining room a soup tureen

serves as a finger bowl and iron stands are incorporated into the «ancestors' armchair» to give it a Gothic look; in the Red Drawing Room the torches of liberty held by the negro slaves are simply upturned candlesticks supporting copper scale pans. Mottoes and inscriptions abound and mirrors are placed so as to enhance the effect of various features.

Hugo used to work on his poems and novels standing at a small table in the **Glass Room** on the third floor overlooking the sea about which he wrote: "there is nothing more peaceful than this creek in calm weather, nothing more tumultuous in a heavy sea. There were ends of branches perpetually wet from the foam. In the spring, it was full of flowers, nests, scents, birds, butterflies and bees." Regularly, he would take a break from his work by going down to Havelet Bay to swim.

From the **Look Out** where he sometimes slept, he could see the house up the road (*La Fallue at 1 Beauregard Lane*) into which his faithful mistress, Juliette Drouot, settled in November 1856. In April 1864 she moved down the road (*n° 20 Hauteville*).

Candie Gardens (Y) – A dramatic statue of the French Romantic poet and novelist Victor Hugo looks out over the sloping lawn. Splendid gardens extend below the museum and the Priaulx Library (formerly Candie House); these were laid out in 1898 as public pleasure gardens with exotic plants (maidenhair tree), replacing the walled orchard and vegetable garden. In the Lower Garden are preserved two glasshouses – the first heated glasshouses to be erected in Guernsey (1792).

Guernsey Museum (YM) – A cluster of modern octagonal structures arranged alongside a former Victorian bandstand (now a tearoom),

houses the Lukis archeological collection of artefacts retrieved from La Varde chambered tomb in 1811 and the Wilfred Carey Collection of paintings, prints and ceramics. The re-creation of a Victorian domestic interior features the pioneer archeologist and eclectic antiquarian collector Frederick Corbin Lukis and his daughter Mary Anne. Certain items were assembled by Wilfred Carey who served several years as a diplomat in the Far East.

An excellent display traces the chronological development of Guernsey complete with geological, archeological and natural history exhibits from the earliest settlers, through the ages to the modern day – the broad range of information given is further supplemented by touch-screens.

Other buildings (Z) – **Elizabeth College (B)**, the public school for boys, was founded as a grammar school in 1563 by Elizabeth I to foster a supply of local English-speaking clergymen. The pseudo-Tudor style building by John Wilson dates from 1826-29.

The elegant neo-Classical Church of **St James's**, designed by John Wilson in 1818 for services held in English for the British garrison, is now a concert hall.

The law courts and the States of Deliberation hold their sittings in the elegant **Royal Court House** (1792); its archives go back 400 years.

■ Excursions
Saumarez Park★

From St Peter Port take the main road (St Julian's Avenue) uphill opposite the harbour; continue straight past the St Pierre Park Hotel on the left, and straight over at the crossroads with Rectory Hill (left) and La Rue du Friquet (right). Follow the one-way system by bearing left, turning right and immediately left (sign) on La Route de Côbo. From the car park walk back parallel with the main road to reach the museum.

The trees and shrubs of this beautiful park are matched by the formal rose gardens; the pond is alive with wildfowl. The **Battle of Flowers** is held here every year on the fourth Thursday in August; most of the floats which compete in the different classes are now made of paper flowers, although real flowers grown locally are still used in some areas and for small floats.

The house **(St John's Residential Home)** dates from 1721 and was the home of Admiral Lord James de Saumarez.

Guernsey Folk Museum★ – Inside the farmstead buildings of Saumarez House are recreated a series of Victorian interiors: downstairs, the kitchen and parlour, heated by a great open fireplace fuelled by seaweed, dung or furze, were known as *la tchuisaene* which, in dialect, alludes to it being the heart of the family home; upstairs are the bedrooms and nursery. Carefully selected period furniture and furnishings are complemented by the fascinating and unusual, old-fashioned accoutrements (kettles, cauldrons) and toys. Elsewhere are displayed a selection of clothes and textiles retrieved in excellent condition from grandmothers' attic chests. Across the courtyard, additional outbuildings display items from the **Langlois Collection of Agricultural Implements** used to furnish a washroom, dairy, cider barn, plough shed – with illustrations and explanations of the different harvesting methods applied to gathering parsnips, potatoes, wheat and corn given in the room above. Other traditional tools common to the quarrymen, tin-smith, blacksmith, cooper, wheelwright, carpenter are also preserved.

Little Chapel

© Guernsey.com

Castel

From St Peter Port take the main road (St Julian's Avenue) uphill opposite the harbour; continue straight past the St Pierre Park Hotel on the left, and turn left down Castle Hill/Les Rohais de Haut. The church is on the right before the crossroads.

Parish Church – Early documents list the Church of St Mary of the Castle (**Ste Marie du Castel** or Our Lady of Deliverance) as belonging to the Abbey of Mont St Michel in 1155; before then, the site may have had a pre-Christian sanctuary and Roman fort, hence its rectangular churchyard.

The 12C church contains 13C frescoes of *The Last Supper* and of the fable of *The Three Living Kings and The Three Dead* – represented by three men hawking on horseback and three skeletal figures *(timed lightswitch next to the organ)*.

Outside the church entrance stands a granite statue menhir found beneath the chancel in 1878. It represents a female figure, probably the mother-goddess of the Neolithic and Bronze Age cults; the stone seats were probably used at the former medieval court of Fief St Michael.

Fine **views** extend to the coast and across to Vale Church.

St Andrew

From St Peter Port take the main road (St Julian's Avenue) uphill opposite the harbour; bear left onto Queen's Road and continue straight on Mount Row/Le Vauquiedor/Mauxmarquis Road, after passing the church (left) turn left to the German Underground Hospital (sign).

German Underground Hospital and Ammunition Store – *La Vassalerie*. *20min*. This is the most extensive project undertaken by the Germans during their occupation of Guernsey: it took nearly three and a half years to build and consists of a series of tunnels, covering an area of 75 000sq ft, excavated from 45-75ft down into the granite bed-rock. When complete, the 500-bed hospital section was used for only nine months to treat French casualties wounded in action against the Liberating Forces. Today the miles of hollow corridor and interlocking wards echo with dripping water, one's own footsteps and silent thoughts: ducts from the central heating and air-conditioning units rust in the confined emptiness, rows of narrow hospital beds furnish the odd ward, signs identify each department: operating theatre, X-ray room, and laboratory **(9)**; dispensary **(2)**; staff sleeping quarters; store rooms; cinema **(15)**; mortuary **(16)**...

Return to the main road, turn left and drive west; as the road descends, turn right (sign) to the Little Chapel and Guernsey Clockmakers.

Little Chapel★ – *Les Vauxbelets*. *20min*. Nestling in a shrubbery, "The Unknown Little Jewel" is a unique model of the grotto and shrine at Lourdes. It was the third in fact to be built in 1925 by Brother Deodat, a Salesian monk from Les Vauxbelets College. Its clinker walls are faced, within and without, with a brilliant mosaic of shells, fragments of glass and bone china: much of which flooded to the site following an article in *The Daily Mirror*.

■ Tour of the island
① Clos Du Valle: St Peter Port to Vale Church
5mi/8km – Half a day

Until 1806 the northern part of Guernsey, known as Clos du Valle, was cut off by the Braye du Valle – a tidal channel of mud-flats and salt-marsh, now protected as a nature reserve, which runs from St Sampson to Grand Havre.

The channel was crossed by a bridge in St Sampson and by a causeway at low water near Vale Church. For reasons of military security it was filled in by Sir John

Doyle; the area of reclaimed salt-pans and mud-flats (300 acres) is now covered with glasshouses. The Clos du Valle is densely populated owing to the many quarries which were worked in the area in the 19C.

Leave St Peter Port by the coast road (Glategny Esplanade) north towards St Sampson. Turn left in Belle Greve Bay into Le Grand Bouet and then second right.

Château des Marais – The ruined medieval **Castle in the Marshes** crowns a low knoll: it was first used in the Bronze Age, protected by the surrounding marshy ground. An outer wall encloses a ditch and inner fortification. Excavations in 1975-77 uncovered 13C coins in a chapel dedicated to Our Lady of the Marshes. The castle was re-fortified in the 18C and was later known as Ivy Castle owing to the creeper which covered it.

St Sampson – Guernsey's second port, which has taken all bulk cargoes since 1964, lies at the eastern end of the Braye du Valle *(see below)*. Shipbuilding in the 18C was eclipsed as the main industry in the 19C by the export of granite for road building; the first of the handsome granite quays was built in 1820. The harbour and its environs feature in Hugo's novel *The Toilers of the Sea* as La Durande.

The first **bridge** originally spanned the Braye du Valle *(see below)*: when it became blocked in 1806, it was faced with stone to form a mooring.

St Sampson, the oldest church in Guernsey, was allegedly built where the saint came ashore (c 550) either from Llantwit Major in South Wales or from Dol in Brittany. The oldest section is the early-Norman saddleback tower. Its attractive churchyard overlooks the disused Longue Hougue Quarry.

Defensive towers

In 1778-79 the shoreline of Guernsey was re-inforced by a chain of 15 loopholed granite towers (30ft/9m high, 20ft/6m in diameter, with walls 4ft/1.22m thick). The 12 that survive, numbered in an anticlockwise sequence, illustrate how advanced they were for their period – an adapted design was later used when similar towers were built in Jersey. The ground level was used for storage; entrance to the first floor was by a retractable wooden ladder and gave access to two levels of accommodation loopholed for musketry defence; the open roof was subsequently altered to make room for a 12-pounder gun. The shortcomings of the design, however, were soon realised by Royal Engineers who advocated a different format for the Martello Towers built at Fort Saumarez, Fort Grey and Fort Hommet (1804), in keeping with those being constructed on the south coast of England.

Detached magazines were built alongside in which kegs or barrels of black powder would be stored protected from the damp sea winds and where muskets could be serviced.

From The Bridge take Vale Avenue north and bear left onto the main road (La Route du Braye). Oatlands Craft Centre is located opposite a garden centre in Gigandis Road.

Oatlands Craft Centre – *Braye Road, St Sampson.* An old brick farmstead and its thatched outbuildings arranged around a courtyard house a craft centre where craftsmen exercise their skills in cheesemaking, goldsmithing, silversmithing and engraving. The two distinctive kilns were used from 1800 to the 1930s to produce bricks for fortifications, chimneys and boiler pits for heating glasshouses, and clay pots for tomatoes.

Vale Castle – The medieval castle, now in ruins, was built on the site of an Iron Age hillfort (c 600 BC) on the only high point in Clos du Valle, overlooking St Sampson harbour. Most of the extant masonry dates from work undertaken after the American Wars of Independence, when France ratified her alliance with the independent American colony and it was considered necessary to consolidate artillery defences and provide additional barracks. These were used by the Island's Militia and by Russian troops evacuated from Holland at the end of the 18C.

There is a fine **view** inland, along the east coast and out to sea to the reef, Alderney *(north)*, Herm and Sark *(west)* and Jersey *(south)*.

Bordeaux Harbour provides mooring for fishing boats; the sheltered bay, which provides the only safe swimming in the area, is described by Victor Hugo in his novel *The Toilers of the Sea.*

Follow the main road north; as it curves gently left, turn right onto the minor road; bear left; park by the dilapidated glasshouses (right) opposite the passage tomb.

Dehus Dolmen – *Light switch on left inside the entrance.* This, the second largest passage grave in Guernsey, has four side-chambers covered by seven capstones: crouch down to see Le Gardien du Tombeau, the figure of an archer *(switch for spotlight)*. It was first excavated in 1837 by Lukis whose finds are in the Guernsey Museum in St Peter Port.

Several minor roads meander northwards to the coast.

Beaucette Quarry Marina – A breach was blasted in the side of this old diorite quarry to turn it into a sheltered marina. Even at high tide only the tops of the masts can be seen.

Fort Doyle★ – From the fort there is an excellent **view** of the Casquets reef and Alderney *(north)*, the French coast, Herm and Sark *(west)*.

Fort Le Marchant – This promontory is the most northerly point in Guernsey. The fort is named after the founder of the Royal Military College at Sandhurst in England. Fine view, particularly of L'Ancresse Bay and L'Ancresse Common.

L'Ancresse Bay – The bay is very popular for bathing and surfing particularly at the western end near Fort Pembroke.

L'Ancresse Common – This is the only extensive open space on the island and is much used for strolling, walking the dog, horse racing, cattle grazing, kite flying and as a golf course. The area is rich in archeological sites: **La Varde Dolmen** is the largest passage grave in Guernsey; human bones and limpet shells were found beneath the six capstones. **Les Fouaillages** burial ground is 7 000 years old; excavations as recent as 1978-81 produced very interesting material. The coastline is well defended by forts and seven defensive towers.

Vale Church – St Michael du Valle was consecrated in 1117 on the site of an earlier chapel dedicated to St Magloire, who with St Sampson brought Christianity to Guernsey in the 6C. Until the end of the 19C the church stood at the edge of a tidal inlet, the Braye du Valle which divided the Clos du Valle from the main island. The church is irregular in alignment, suggesting that it was built in stages by

Benedictine monks from Mont St Michel who had founded a priory nearby in 968; the priory was in ruins by 1406 and finally demolished in 1928.

Inside, the chancel is decorated with Arts and Crafts tiles; the window in the Archangel Chapel is from the William Morris studio; to the right of the altar is an unusually large piscina.

Outside stands a 7C monument unearthed in 1949 beyond the west door. In the churchyard rest a number of pirates and smugglers shipwrecked nearby.

Past the southeast corner of the Vale churchyard runs the Military Road, the first to be built by Sir John Doyle, which crosses the island north of St Peter Port to the east coast.

② West Coast: Grand Havre to Pezeries Point

10mi/15km – About half a day

The **Grand Havre**, an ample inlet at the west end of the Braye du Valle, is best admired from the Rousse headland with its tower and jetty. A more extensive horizon, including the many sandy bays which scallop the west coast in both directions, is visible from the German gun battery strategically situated on the granite headland, the **Grandes Rocques**.

Côbo Bay★★ – The bay is a charming combination of sand for swimming and surfing, and rocks for exploring marine life.

Vazon Bay – The huge beach between Fort Houmet (*north*) and Fort le Crocq (*south*) is excellent

La Chevauchée de St Michel

Until 1837 this medieval ceremony, which probably originated in pagan Normandy, took place every three years just before the Feast of Corpus Christi with its procession of the blessed sacrament. The cavalcade (*chevauchée*) consisted of the Crown Officers and the officials of the feudal court of St Michel du Valle who made a tour of inspection of the island highways; they were dressed in costume and mounted on horseback, armed with a sword and attended by one or two footmen (*pions*). The *pions* were usually handsome bachelors and it was their privilege to kiss any young women they met. They lunched at Pezeries; dinner was provided out of the fines levied on the owners of any obstructions; Le Perron du Roi near to the Forest Church served as a mounting block for dignitaries.

for swimming, sunbathing, surfing, horse riding and motor and motorcycle racing. Beneath the sands lie the remains of a submerged forest; at dusk, the rocks assume animal-like shapes such as lions and camels.

St Apolline's Chapel★ – In 1394 a charter was granted for a chantry chapel which is decorated with a **fresco** *(light switch)* of *The Last Supper*. The original dedication to Ste Marie de la Perelle was changed in 1452 to St Apolline (or St Apollonia), whose cult became very popular in Europe at that time. She was an elderly deaconess who was burned to death in an anti-Christian riot in Alexandria in 249; as she was first struck repeatedly in the face and lost many teeth she is invoked against toothache; she is often represented bearing forceps.

After the Reformation the chapel was used as a barn; it was restored in 1978.

Le Trépied Dolmen – This burial chamber at the southern end of Perelle Bay was excavated in 1840 by Frederic Lukis, whose finds are in the Guernsey Museum. In past centuries the site was used for witches' Sabbaths on Friday nights.

L'Erée Headland – The tall defensive tower on the headland is called Fort Saumarez. To the south stands **Le Creux ès Faies Dolmen**, a passage grave said locally to be the entrance to Fairyland; other local myths talk of it being a meeting place for witches. Excavation has produced items dating from 2000-1800 BC.

Table des Pions

Lihou island – *Accessible by causeway at low tide; check tide tables before setting out and take note of the time for returning to the main island.* The semi-detached character of the island is inviting to those seeking the contemplative life. In 1114 a priory was founded and dedicated to Our Lady of the Rock (now in ruins). Earlier this century there was a burst of activity from a factory making iodine from seaweed. The predecessor of the present lonely farmhouse was used by the Germans for target practice. On the west coast a 100ft rock pool provides excellent bathing.

Rocquaine Bay* – The grand sweep of the bay, which is protected from erosion by a high sea wall, is interrupted by the Cup and Saucer, originally a medieval fort to which a defensive tower was added in 1804. It is painted white as a navigation mark.

Fort Grey Maritime Museum – The tower presently accommodates a small museum on two floors dedicated to the history of the fort, and to the many shipwrecks in Guernsey waters, the Hanois Reef and Lighthouse; displays also include artefacts salvaged by marine archeologists from a hundred ships which have run aground along the west coast between 1750 and 1978 – a video explains the disaster involving the loss of the *Orion* and the ensuing difficult rescue operation.

Portelet – The picturesque harbour full of fishing boats is backed by the houses of the Hanois Lighthouse keepers. Nearby is the **Table des Pions**, a circle of turf surrounded by a ditch and a ring of stones, where the *pions* or footmen of the Chevauchée de St Michel ate their lunch sitting at the grass table with their feet in the trench.

Pezeries Point** – This is the most westerly point in all the Channel Islands, a remote and unfrequented place. The fort was built in the Napoleonic era.

③ Southern Cliffs: Pleinmont Point to St Peter Port

16mi/26km – Half a day

These cliffs which extend along the south coast and round to St Peter Port provide some of the most wild and dramatic scenery in the island *(beware of the cliff face which can be unstable and dangerous)*; a footpath runs from the western end to the town, following the contours up and down the valleys and bays.

Pleinmont Point – The headland which is crowned by TV masts provides an extensive **view**: along the southern cliffs *(east)*, out to the Hanois Lighthouse and its surrounding reefs *(west)*, across Rocquaine Bay to Lihou Island *(north)*. The headland is still dominated by a coastal artillery direction-finding tower with wide observation openings, imposed by the Germans upon an existing Martello Tower: others were constructed at Fort Saumarez, Chouet, La Corbière and L'Angle.

© Gernsey.com

Torteval Parish Church

Renoir in Guernsey

The French Impressionist painter spent a month in Guernsey late in 1883, during which time he painted some 15 canvases with views of the bay and beach of Moulin Huet – heralded in contemporary guidebooks as the island's finest scenic attraction. Little is known of the reasons why Renoir visited the island – which Hugo later described as having "the singular attraction of combining a climate made for leisure with a population made for toil". For the Victorian Englishman, the place provided idyllic holiday conditions blessed with a gentle climate and exotic vegetation including the sweetest grapes, ripened under glass and harvested from July to September. For the French, Guernsey was a secluded retreat from the bustle of the Brittany coastal resorts.

From here to La Moye Point the cliffs are bare and rugged, indented by small bays and inlets and pierced by many caves. A footpath stretches all along the clifftops through National Trust land, past all the watch houses before coming out by the Aquarium in St Peter Port.

The roof of a cave in La Forge Bay has fallen in to form a **blow-hole** (*souffleur*); the best time to see and hear it in action is about 2 hours after low tide.

La Moye Point, the smallest of the three promontories on the south coast, is wild and beautiful. Le Gouffre, a charming steep valley, flanks it on the west. On the east side precipitous steps lead down to a three-tiered mooring for fishing boats in the shelter of the headland.

Return to the main road (La Route de Pleinmont); continue east towards St Peter Port; Torteval Church is on the left.

Torteval – The unusual name of Guernsey's smallest parish is thought to derive from the twisting valley that runs down to Fort Grey. The original Church of St Philippe was demolished in 1816. The present church, intended as a Calvinist chapel is very plain – its distinctive round spire being its most interesting feature.

Take La Rue de la Villiaze which bear right onto La Rue des Landes; turn right towards Forest Church (St Margaret's or Ste Marguérite de la Forêt) and then left or right around it (sign: German Occupation Museum).

German Occupation Museum – *1hr*. This museum has grown out of a private collection of artefacts from the Nazi occupation of the Channel Islands. A short video *(7min)* serves as an introduction to the period of occupation. A series of rooms displays various aspects of life at that time: military hardware (weaponry, radio telephones); vehicles; clothing, uniforms and associated paraphernalia (badges, buttons, mending kits); a field kitchen, food parcels, food substitutes and rationing; personal mementoes of German soldiers and forced labourers, newspapers and posters; video of the occupation and the liberation. All vehicles and mechanical artefacts are carefully maintained in working order – hence the smell of motor oil!

Either take one of a number of small roads leading south to the coast, or return to the main road and turn right, as if to the Manor Hotel, to Petit Bot Bay.

Petit Bot Bay – This attractive bay which has good bathing and sand at low water lies at the foot of a green valley guarded by a defensive tower (1780). The stream used to turn a corn and a paper mill but they and two hotels were destroyed by the Germans after a British Commando raid in July 1940.

Return uphill to the main road; turn right down La Rue de la Villette, which turns inland to rejoin the valley leading down to Moulin Huet Bay.

Icart Point★★ – This is the highest and most southerly headland with very fine **views** of the coast. The view west reveals a string of quiet sandy beaches, some difficult of access, curving round to La

Moye Point. On the east side is **Saint's Bay**, a favourite mooring for fishermen.

Moulin Huet Bay – A water lane runs down the valley, one of the most beautiful in Guernsey, to the bay where the stream plunges down the cliff face to the sea. This is where the French Impressionist painter **Renoir** used to come (1883), fascinated by the rocks that glow pink in the setting sun. Both this bay and its eastern neighbour are good for bathing but the sandy beach at **Petit Port** is superior.

St Martin – The parish occupies the southeast section of Guernsey and is principally residential, well-served by former military roads to its jagged coastline.

La Gran'mère du Chimquière★ – At the gate into St Martin's church-yard stands a Stone Age menhir carved to represent a female figure; her facial features were chiselled later. Known as the Grandmother of the Cemetery, she is supposed to guarantee fertility and receives gifts of coins and flowers. The statue was broken in two in the 19C by an over-zealous churchwarden but re-erected by the parishioners. The church itself dates from 1225-50; the south porch was added in the 1520s. Inside, it has a pre-Reformation font; the lectern and oak pulpit are worked in the Breton style and date from 1657.

Return to the main road; turn right to Jerbourg.

La Gran'mère
du Chimquière

The road passes the **Doyle Column** which commemorates Sir John Doyle, Lt Governor (1803-15); plaque showing distances to other islands. From here the clifftop footpath provides some spectacular views through the pine trees of the coastline. At the southern tip sit the Pea Stacks – the third outcrop of rock, resembling the form of a monk, is called Le Petit Bonhomme Andriou.

The ramparts of a Bronze Age hillfort still crown the headland *(beyond the car park)* together with the remains of 20C German gun batteries.

St Martin's Point★★ – There is a magnificent **view** down to the lighthouse on the point, north up the coast to St Peter Port and seaward to the other islands.

Jerbourg Point★ – From the Pea Stacks rising from the sea just off the point the view swings northwest into the broad sweep of Moulin Huet Bay. The Jerbourg peninsula is the southeastern extremity of Guernsey: it was inhabited as early as Neolithic times; during the Bronze Age earthern ramparts and ditches were reinforced and in the Middle Ages, when Castle Cornet was occupied by the French a defensive castle, the Château de Jerbourg, was built here to shelter islanders through troubles.

Fermain Bay – *Access on foot from car park or cliff path from Jerbourg.* This charming bay with its pebbled cove, backed by densely wooded cliffs and an 18C defensive tower, offers a sandy beach and good bathing at low tide. The pepperpot tower is a Napoleonic sentry box. At low spring tides the remains of German anti-landing barriers can be discerned.

Continue east on the main road; on a lefthand curve, turn left beyond main gate into shaded car park.

Sausmarez Manor – 1hr. The elegant Queen Anne house was built in 1714-18 by Sir Edmund Andros, the Seigneur of Sausmarez and former Governor of New York. The roof-top "widow's walk" is a traditional East Coast American feature implemented to provide a view far out to sea. The later Regency additions at the rear were largely rebuilt in the 1870s by General George de Sausmarez who served with the East India Company.

The welcoming interior displays portraits and souvenirs of 750 years of occupation by the Seigneurs of Sausmarez: fine antique tapestries hang in the dark and cosy dining room; handsome family furniture and objects are scattered through the spacious drawing room and larger dining room; the log of the round-the-world voyage of *HMS Centurion* in which Philip Saumarez served is kept with the

Inca silver from a captured Spanish treasure ship which was turned into coin of the realm in the great beamed hall...

In an outbuilding are displayed a **collection of dolls' houses**, several of which meticulously recreate typical Guernsey household interiors.

The wooded **grounds** are planted with various strains of tall bamboo and camellias. The **sculpture park** displays a beautiful and comprehensive range of work by artists from many countries – to be admired, enjoyed and purchased; works may also be commissioned.

The park gates, with sculptures by Sir Henry Cheere, celebrate the return of the Manor to the de Sausmarez branch of the family in 1748.

Fort George – This modern luxury housing estate occupies the site of the British garrison, Fort George, built from 1782 to 1812 and destroyed by Allied bombers the day before D-Day, having been adapted by the Germans to serve as the war-time headquarters of the Luftwaffe early-warning service. The garrison troops used to bathe in the sea below, hence the name Soldiers' Bay. The military cemetery on the clifftop below the fort harbours the only German war graves still on the island.

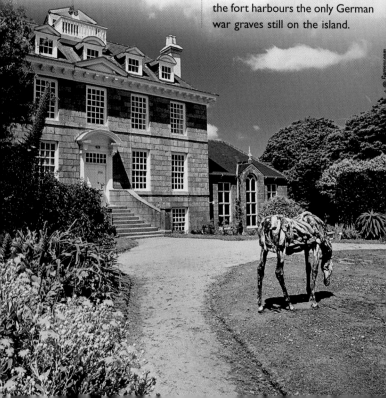

As the main road descends towards the waterfront, turn sharp right (sign: Aquarium).

La Valette Underground Military Museum – The museum occupies five tunnels that were excavated to hold fuel tanks *(Höhlgang)* for refuelling U-boats: one tunnel was never completed. The four metal containers in situ at the end of the occupation were manufactured in Bremen, and had a capacity of 30 000 gallons; on examination they were found to contain a kind of oil extracted from coal. Today the area has been adapted to accommodate displays of uniforms and apparel belonging to the Guernsey Militia (officially constituted in 1203); German artefacts and mementoes of the occupation.

Guernsey Aquarium – Installed in a disused tunnel is a series of water tanks housing a variety of aquatic creatures: tropical and indigenous fish, conger eels, sharks, lobsters, reptiles and amphibians. The tunnel housing them was excavated in 1860 to carry a tramway south along the coast; work was abandoned after a rock fall; the Germans extended it in 1940-45. ■

Sausmarez Manor

ALDERNEY

Alderney is the most northerly of the Channel Islands and lies west (8mi/12km) of the tip of the Cherbourg Peninsula in Normandy, separated from the Cap de la Hague headland by the treacherous tidal current known to sailors as the **Alderney Race**. The island (3.5mi long by 1.5mi wide) slopes gently from a plateau (296ft/90m)

Population 2 297
Michelin Atlas p 5 or Map 503

of farmland, skirted by high cliffs in the southwest, to a tongue of low-lying land in the northeast, fringed by rocky spits and sandy bays, and bristling with redundant fortifications.

There is one main settlement, St Anne's, also known as The Town, which extends north towards the coast and the harbour; there are a few outlying dwellings, some in former military forts

Alderney is a haven for nature-lovers. The flora includes wild broom, thrift, sea campion, ox-eye daisies, wild orchids and the bastard toad-flax (thesium humifusum); among the fauna are black rabbits and blonde hedgehogs. Birdwatchers have much to choose from - hoopoes and golden orioles, birds of prey and the occasional white stork or purple heron, and the sea-birds, fulmars, guillemots and kittiwakes, especially the colonies of gannets and puffins. At low tide the rock pools reveal a variety of marine life; anemones, corals and ormers.

Constitution – Alderney is part of the Bailiwick of Guernsey. Since the introduction of the new constitution on 1 January 1949, the budget and other financial matters have to be approved by the States of Guernsey. Otherwise all island business is decided by the Committees of the States of Alderney,

Practical Information

Tourist Information Centre – www.alderney.gov.gg

Victoria Street, St Anne ☎ 01481 823 737; States Office, PO Box 1, Queen Elizabeth II Street, Alderney GY9 3AA ☎ 01481 822 811; Fax 01481 822 436; tourism@alderney.net

Access – By air or sea. See p 111.

Alderney Airport – ☎ 01481 822 888

Alderney Harbour Office – ☎ 01481 822 620.

Taxis and Buses – Passengers disembarking at the Harbour may find excursion coaches or taxis waiting for a fare; taxis may also be found waiting at the airport, completed in 1935, but coaches must be booked. Both the harbour and the airport are only 10min on foot from St Anne's.

J S Taxis ☎ 01481 823 181, Mob 07781 100 830

A B C Taxis ☎ 01481 823760

Island Taxis ☎ 01481 823 823

Island Bus Service – During the summer months there is a bus service following a circular route from Butes car park via the harbour and camp site to Longis Bay, returning via the town.

Guided Tours – There is a guided tour of the island every afternoon, a round trip by bus or coach from the taxi rank in Victoria Street, with two stops: first at Fort Albert and then on the cliffs at Giffoine (west coast) to see the gannets on Les Etacs.

Vehicle and Cycle Hire – The road network may be very limited but there are several vehicle hire companies. As the distances are not great, cycling is an excellent way to explore the island. Several companies hire out bicycles for adults and children.

Alderney Car and Moped Hire ☎ 01481 823 352

Bray Hire Cars (also mini mokes) ☎ 01481 823 881

Central Car Hire (also mini mokes and battery powered cycles) ☎ 01481 822 971

Pedal Power, Les Roquettes ☎ 01481 822 286

J B Cycles, Val Reuter Garages ☎ 01481 822 294 or 822 762

Puffin Cycles ☎ 01481 823 725

Top Gear, Le Banquage ☎ 01481 822 000

Alderney Railway – The only standard-gauge railway to survive in the Channel Islands, which was opened in 1847 to carry sandstone to the harbour, is now operated by the Alderney Railway Society, formed in 1978; steam and diesel trains run from Braye Road to Mannez Quarry.

Forts Tour – The tours include both the Victorian and German fortifications.

Boat trips – In summer there are trips from Braye Harbour round Alderney (2 hr) and round Burhou Island, and charter trips to the other islands or to France (passports required) provided by two small vessels – *The Voyager* and *Lady Maris*.

The Volyager, McAllister's Fish Shop, Victoria Street ☎ 823 666; Mob 07781 160 260

Lady Maris, Alderney Gift Box, Victoria Street ☎ 823 632; Mob 07781 100 840

Beaches – Good sandy beaches safe for swimming – Braye Bay, Saye Bay, Arch Bay, Corblets Bay, Longis Bay, Telegraph Bay (except at high tide) – and many which are suitable for watersports, particularly sail-boarding and surfing.

Sailing – Braye Harbour offers safe moorings and good anchorage and on-shore facilities (showers, toilets, laundry, chandlery, marine engineers, petrol, diesel fuel, calor gas, camping gaz). Navigational advice and weather reports available from the Harbourmaster.

Sea-angling – There is a tackle shop in St Anne; the local angling club holds an annual festival in October. Summer visitors are likely to catch mackerel, garfish, wrasse, pollack, plaice, sole and bass; later in the season come mullet, conger and tope.

Walking – The island is best explored on foot – about the town, across the common, along the beaches or the cliffs (take care on the cliff-top paths and do not attempt to descend the cliff face).

Golf – 9 hole course. Golf clubs available for hire.

Alderney Week – The week-long Festival (early August) includes flower-decorated floats, daft-raft races, a man-powered flight competition from the sea wall, fancy dress and fashion competitions, children's races, knockout cricket and tug-of-war contests, and culminates in a torchlight procession, bonfire and firework display.

Places to Stay – There are hotels and bed-and-breakfast places, as well as self-catering. Camping facilities are available at the Saye Camp Site, on the edge of Saye Bay ☎ 01481 822 556.

Aderney Hotels and Guest House Association – www.internet. alderney.gg/beds

☎ 01481 824 242 ; Fax 01481 823 650; tourism@alderny.net

Beds Hotline – www.internet.alderney.gg/beds

☎ 01481 824 242; Fax 01481 823 650; tourism@alderney.net

See the Practical Information chapter for other suggestions on where to stay.

Places to Eat – The menus feature freshly-caught seafood as well as pub snacks and barbecues. The gastronomic high point of the year is the Annual Seafood Festival Week, held in May.

See the Practical Information chapter for other suggestions on where to eat.

Licensed Premises – Pub opening hours are from 10am to 12.30am. Children are welcome with their parents. On Milk-o-Punch Sunday in May a drink of milk, eggs and rum is offered free of charge by the pub-licans of the island.

which consists of 10 elected members and an elected President, who serve for four years. The Court consists of six Jurats under a Chairman, who are appointed by the Home Office.

The pre-1949 constitution which had evolved down the centuries included two other bodies, the Douzaine, an assembly of 12 heads of families, and the Court of Chief Pleas. All offices were then elective. The feudal system under a seigneur was never established in Alderney; later Governors, appointed by the Crown from the 16C to the 19C, often met with opposition from the independent-minded islanders.

Economy – Two constants in the economy of Alderney are fishing and farming; providing the visitor with a delicious variety of fresh fish and crustaceans; before the Second World War this was supplemented by income from exporting cattle, granite and gravel. Tourism, which began after the defeat of Napoleon when people came to visit the many retired military personnel who settled on the island, was given a boost when Queen Victoria inspected the fortifications in 1854.

Alderney supports a small prosperous community, a significant portion of which has settled there since the Second World War. The atmosphere is friendly as the residents know each other and are happy to welcome visitors in search of a quiet holiday away from the more sophisticated and popular resorts. There is also a burgeoning off-shore financial sector based on e-commerce and IT.

Historical notes – Owing to its key position, nearest to England, France and the Channel shipping lanes, Alderney has frequently been fortified. The Romans seem to have used it as a naval base; there are traces of a late-Roman fort at the Nunnery. The first English fortifications date from the reign of Henry VIII who started to construct a fort on the hill south of Longis Bay. Faced with the threat of invasion in the Napoleonic period, the British Government strengthened the existing defences and sent a garrison of 300 to assist the local militia.

The most impressive fortifications were built between 1847 and 1858. Alarmed by the development of a French naval base at Cherbourg, the British Government decided to create a safe harbour at Braye, by constructing a huge breakwater, and to defend the island, by building a chain of 10 forts along the north coast from Clonque in the west round to Longis Bay in the east. There was also a plan to build another harbour at Longis and link it to Braye with a canal, thus strengthening the defence of the northeastern sector and providing a safe harbour whatever the wind.

The forts were constructed of local stone with white quoins and dressings; several stood offshore and were reached by causeways at low tide.

In June 1940 almost all the population left the island and the livestock was evacuated to Guernsey. During their five-year occupation the Germans re-fortified most of the Victorian forts and built masses of ugly concrete fortifications. When the islanders began to return late in 1945 they found their possessions gone and the houses derelict or destroyed. It took 10 years and substantial government aid to make good the damage.

■ St Anne

The charm of St Anne lies in its cobbled streets and smart whitewashed granite houses; its appearance is reminiscent of villages in Cornwall and Normandy. The Town, as it is called by the islanders, lies about half a mile from the north coast on the edge of the best agricultural land, known as La Blaye.

The original medieval settlement of farmhouses was centred on **Marais Square** which was then unpaved and had a stream running through it where the washing was done. As in ancient times, narrow lanes or *venelles* lead out to the un-enclosed fields divided into *riages*, each consisting of a number of strips: Alderney is one of the few places in the British Isles still to operate this archaic system of managing open agricultural land, although electric fencing is occasionally used.

Another settlement grew up at **Le Huret**, where the people gathered to decide when to gather the seaweed (*vraic*) used to fertilise the land. In the 15C more houses were built to the east of the square, to accommodate settlers from Guernsey, and the Blaye was extended to support a population of 700. In the 18C the huge profits made from privateering led to a building boom; thatch was replaced by tiles, the first Court House was built and the Governor spent money on improving the communal buildings as well as his own residence. The northern part of the town – **Queen Elizabeth II Street, Victoria Street and Ollivier Street** – developed in the early Victorian era when the population of the island trebled with the introduction of a military garrison and many immigrant labourers brought in to build the harbour. Utilitarian workmen's cottages were built of local sandstone at Newtown and elsewhere. Many attractive houses and gardens line the green lanes, such as La Vallée, which run from St Anne down to the north coast.

St Anne's – The church, consecrated in 1850, was designed by Sir Gilbert Scott in the transitional style from Norman to Early English cruciform and built in local granite dressed with white Caen stone. The cost was borne by Revd Canon John Le Mesurier, son of the last hereditary governor of Alderney, in memory of his parents. The church is unexpectedly large as it was intended to hold not only the local population, then swollen by immigrant labourers, but also the military garrison.

English was then replacing Norman French as the local language; the lectern holds two Bibles, and the texts in the apse and near the door appear in both languages. Below the west window, which shows children of all races, are six brass plaques commemorating the Le Mesurier family who governed the island from 1721 to 1825. Queen Elizabeth II's visit to Alderney in 1957 is recorded in the window in the Lady Chapel.

During the war the church was damaged by being used as a store and the bells were removed; two were recovered on the island and the other four were found in Cherbourg. The churchyard gates in Victoria Street, erected as a memorial to Prince Albert, were removed by the Germans but replaced by a local resident.

Museum – The Alderney Society's Museum presents a comprehensive view of the island: geology; flora and fauna; archeology, particularly finds from the Iron Age Settle-ment at Les Hughettes; domestic and military history, including the Victorian fortifications and the German Occupation.

The collections are displayed in the **old school** which was endowed in 1790 by the Governor *(inscription over the gate)*.

The **Clock Tower** (1767) standing nearby is all that remains of the old church which was pulled down when the present one was built. The original dedication to St Mary, and the name of the town too, was changed to St Anne early in the 17C.

Royal Connaught Square – This elegant square, which was renamed in 1905 on the occasion of a visit by the Duke of Connaught, was the centre of the town in the 18C.

Island Hall *(north side)*, a handsome granite building which is now a community centre and library, was enlarged in 1763 by John Le Mesurier to become Government House. The first house on the site was built by Captain Nicholas Ling, who was appointed Lt Governor in 1657 and lived there until his death in 1679. **Mouriaux House** was completed in 1779 by the Governor as his private residence.

Court House – The present building in Queen Elizabeth II Street (formerly New Street) dates from 1850. Both the Court and the States of Alderney hold their sessions in the first-floor Court Room which was restored in 1955.

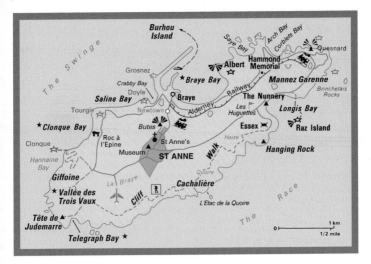

Victoria Street – This, the main shopping street, runs north past the church gates and the war memorial, which records the dead of both World Wars. Its name was changed from Rue du Grosnez to celebrate Queen Victoria's visit in 1854.

Butes – The recreation ground, formerly the Butts, provides fine views of Braye Bay *(northeast)*, across Crabby Bay and the Swinge to the Casquets *(northwest)* and the English Channel.

■ Burhou island

The island, which lies northwest across The Swinge (about 1.5mi/ 2km), is extensively riddled with rabbit warrens and supports large colonies of puffins, razorbills, gannets and storm petrels as well as other sea-birds. A hut provides simple accommodation for an overnight stay for bird-watching.

■ Tour of the island

9mi; 1 day

It is possible to walk round the island following the cliff-top footpath or to drive round making detours on foot to places of interest.

Braye – The harbour is protected by Fort Grosnez (1853) which was built at the same time as the massive **breakwater** (1 000yd long plus another 600yd submerged) by the British Government in 1847, just as the French were consolidating their defences at Cherbourg. As with St Catherine's Bay in Jersey, the ambitious plans for harbours of refuge were never completely realised. The first quay, the Old Jetty, was built in 1736 by the Governor to provide a safe landing stage for the privateers and smugglers he "protected". The modern concrete jetty dates from the turn of the century.

Braye Bay★ – The largest bay on the island offers a sandy beach with good bathing and a fine view of the ferries, yachts and fishing boats in the harbour. Skirting the beach is a strip of grass, Le Banquage, where the seaweed *(vraic)* was left to dry.

Fort Albert – Mount Touraille, at the east end of Braye Bay, is crowned by Fort Albert (1853), the most impressive element in the Victorian chain of forts and German fortifications. From the seaward side there is a fine **view** inland to St Anne, westwards across Braye Bay to Fort Grosnez and the breakwater with Fort Tourgis in the background, and eastwards over the northern end of the island.

Hammond Memorial – *At the fork in the road east of Fort Albert.* The labourers of the Todt Organisation – paid volunteers from Vichy France, political refugees from Franco's Spain, Ukraine, Russia, North Africa who worked under duress on the fortifications during the Nazi Occupation are commemorated in a series of plaques inscribed in the languages of the prisoners. There were three camps on Alderney, each holding 1 500 men.

North Coast – Three excellent sandy bathing bays cluster round the most northerly headland beneath the walls of Fort Chateau à l'Etoc (1854), now converted into private flats: **Saye Bay**, nearly symmetrical in shape; **Arch Bay**, named after the tunnel through which the carts collecting seaweed reached the shore; **Corblets Bay**, overlooked by Fort Corblets (1855), now a private house with a splendid view.

Mannez Garenne – The low-lying northern end of the island, known as Mannez Garenne (Warren) is dominated by the remains of a German Observation Tower on the edge of the quarry.

Quesnard Lighthouse (1912) stands 121ft high and casts its beam nearly 17 miles. From the lantern platform there is a magnificent **view★** of the coast and the Race and, on a clear day, of the nuclear power station on the French coast. Many ships have come to grief on this rocky coast where the strong currents of the Swinge and the Race (Raz) meet. The most famous was the *Liverpool*, which ran aground in a fog in February 1902.

Three forts command the coastline: Les Homeaux Florains (1858), now in ruins, was approached by a causeway; Fort Quesnard, on the east side of Cats Bay, and Fort Houmet Herbe, another offshore fort reached by a causeway, were built in 1853.

Longis Bay – The retreating tide reveals a broad stretch of sand backed by a German tank trap which provides excellent shelter for sunbathing. The shallow bay was the island's natural harbour from prehistoric times until it silted up early in the 18C. Traces of an Iron Age settlement were discovered at **Les Huguettes** in 1968 when the golf course was being laid out on Longis Common; the finds are displayed in the museum. Various relics (coins, tiles, pottery and brickwork) indicate the existence of a Roman naval base protected by a fort (c 2C-4C AD).

Raz Island – A causeway, which is covered at high tide, runs out to the island in the centre of Longis Bay. The fort (1853) has been partially restored and there is a fine **view** of Essex Castle and Hanging Rock *(southwest)*.

© Gensey.com

The Nunnery – This building, which is thought to be the oldest on the island, stands on a rectangular site enclosed within a wall (16ft high). John Chamberlain converted it to his use when he became Governor in 1584. Its name was supplied by the British soldiers who were garrisoned there in the late 18C. It is now private dwellings owned by the States of Alderney.

Essex Castle – The first fort on Essex Hill overlooking Longis Bay was begun in 1546 by Henry VIII but abandoned in 1553. It consisted of an outer bailey, to hold the islanders and their flocks, around a central fort divided into four keeps. All but the north and west sides of the outer wall were razed in 1840 when the present structure was built, to be used first as a barracks and then as a military hospital; it is now private property. The pepperpot gazebo was added by the Governor, John Le Mesurier, who started a farm to feed the garrison at the Nunnery and called it Essex Farm; the name ascended the hill to the castle. At this point, the coastline to the west and south becomes ruggedly rocky.

Hanging Rock – The tilt of the 50ft column of rock projecting from the cliff face is said to have been caused by the people of Guernsey hitching a rope to the rock and trying to tow Alderney away.

Cliff Walk – From Haize round to Giffoine there is a magnificent cliff walk served by frequent paths running inland back to St Anne. The cliff edge is indented by a series of small valleys sloping seaward and a few narrow bays, difficult or impossible of access; bathing is not advisable owing to the swiftly flowing currents in the Race. The view of the steep cliffs plunging into the rock-strewn sea is magnificent.

Cachalière – A path leads down past the old quarry to a pier, built early this century for loading granite but abandoned owing to the dangerous offshore currents. The name derives from Chicago where the Alderney man who paid for the pier had made his fortune. From here the rocks of **L'Etac de la Quoire** can be reached at low water.

Telegraph Bay* – *Access by path and steps, which are not recommended as they are steep and difficult; beware of being cut off from the base of the steps by the rising tide.* The Telegraph Tower (1811), which provided communication with Jersey and Guernsey via a repeating telegraph signal on Sark, has given its name to the bay

Les Casquets

The sandstone reefs lie 7mi west of Alderney, close to the main Channel shipping lane: their name is a corruption of The Cascades, derived, it is thought, from the turbulent waters encountered in the vicinity. The first lighthouses to be built there were powered by coal, then by oil and finally by electricity generated on the reef itself. The present beacon (120ft tall), managed by Trinity House, is clearly visible from Guernsey. Throughout history the Casquets have been a notorious hazard to seamen, most especially when thick fog prevails.

below. Except at high tide there is excellent bathing, sheltered from all but a south wind, and a fine view of La Nache and Fourquie rocks.

Tête de Judemarre – The headland provides a fine **view** of the rock-bound coast and of the islands of Guernsey, Herm and Sark.

Vallée des Trois Vaux★ – This deep cleft is in fact three valleys meeting on a shingle beach.

Giffoine – From the cliff it is possible to see the birds on their nests in the gannet colony on Les Etacs. The remains of a German coastal battery crown the headland above Hannaine Bay, where sandy spits between the rocks provide reasonable bathing. Fine **view** of Burhou, Ortac and the Casquets (north).

Clonque Bay★ – A zigzag path descends the gorse and heather-clad slope above the attractive sweep of the bay. A causeway runs out to Fort Clonque (1855) which was designed by Captain William

Jervois, the same military architect as for most of the other forts on Alderney, now converted into flats belonging to the Landmark Trust. Seaweed from Clonque was highly prized as fertiliser and two causeways enabled the "vraicing" carts to descend to the beds of seaweed.

Just south of Fort Tourgis (1855), now largely derelict, at the northern end of the bay, is the best preserved burial chamber on the island, **Roc à l'Epine**, which consists of a capstone supported on two upright stones. Alderney was once rich in such megaliths but all the others seem to have been destroyed when the Victorian fortifications were built.

Saline Bay – The shore, which is exposed to heavy seas so that bathing can be hazardous, is commanded by a gun battery and Fort Doyle, now a youth centre; beyond lies **Crabby Bay** in the lee of Fort Grosnez. ■

SARK**

Sark, the last feudal fief in Europe and also the smallest independent state in the Commonwealth, offers peace and tranquillity and a traditional way of life without cars. It is located at the very heart of the Channel Islands (7.5mi east of Guernsey, 19mi south of Alderney, 12mi northwest of Jersey). Its two parts – Great Sark and Little Sark – are linked by La Coupée, a high narrow neck of land which inspired Turner, Swinburne and Mervyn Peake, who set the closing scenes of his novel *Mr Pye* here.

Population 550
Michelin Atlas p 5 or Map 503

The island (3.5mi long by 1.5mi wide) consists of a green plateau bounded by high granite cliffs dropping sheer into the sea or flanking sheltered bays and sandy beaches. Many walks give access to the spectacular coastal scenery. Sark is a haven for wildlife – marine creatures in the rock pools and caves; a wide range of bird species; wild flowers in spring and summer.

Constitution – At its head is the hereditary Lord (seigneur) who holds the fief of Sark; the present holder is Michael Beaumont, grandson of Sybil Hathaway, the Dame of Sark, whose long reign from 1927 to 1974 saw the island through difficult and changing times. The Seigneur of Sark has retained a number of privileges from the feudal period: the right to keep pigeons and to own a bitch. He also receives one-thirteenth of the sale price of all island property.

Sark has its own parliament, the Chief Pleas, composed of the 40 tenants and 12 deputies elected for three years. The Seneschal is responsible for justice, together with the Clerk of the Court (Greffier) and the Sheriff (Prévôt). Law and order are upheld by the Constable assisted by the Vingtenier. A person under arrest is held in the tiny prison (2 cells) for 48 hours. In summer the local force is supplemented by a policeman from Guernsey. Serious cases are heard by the Guernsey courts.

History – In the middle of the 6C St Magloire, the nephew of St Sampson, landed in Sark from Brittany with 62 companions and founded a monastery. In the 9C the island was prey to Viking raids but little is known of the island's history before it became part of the Duchy of Normandy.

© Guernsey.com

View from
Point Robert

In 1042 Sark was given to the Abbey of Mont St Michel by William the Conqueror, the Duke of Normandy. A few years later the island was attached to the diocese of Coutances. In 1336 Sark was invaded by a party of Scotsmen under David Bruce, a king in exile. Two years later Sark was attacked by Frenchmen. In 1349 the monks abandoned the island and for several years it was a lawless place, the haunt of pirates. The French regained it in 1549 but were thrown out by an Anglo-Dutch force which returned it to England.

In 1565 Elizabeth I granted Sark to Helier de Carteret, Lord of the Manor of St Ouen in Jersey, on condition that he establish a colony of 40 settlers prepared to defend the island. Helier became the first Lord of Sark who set about dividing the land into 40 holdings, attributing one to each of the 40 families who had accompanied him from Jersey, on condition that each tenant build and maintain a house and provide an armed man to defend the island. The number of holdings has not changed since then.

The island of Brecqhou (just off the west coast across the Gouliot Passage) has been a dependent of the fiefdom of Sark since 1565; it is now on perpetual lease to the reclusive multi-millionaire Barclay twins who have built a massive neo-Gothic mansion, which they rarely visit.

■ Tour of the island *1 day*

Great Sark

Maseline Harbour – The lighthouse (1912) looks down over the harbour from the cliffs on Point Robert as the boat docks inside the modern concrete jetty, which was inaugurated in 1949 by the Duke of Edinburgh when he and the then Princess Elizabeth visited Sark.

Creux Harbour★ – Opposite the tunnel to Maseline Harbour is a second tunnel to Creux Harbour, an older and picturesque little harbour, which is dry at low tide.

La Collinette – A short tunnel leads to Harbour Hill *(0.5mi);* at the top is the crossroads called La Collinette.

Straight ahead stretches **The Avenue**, once the drive to the original manor house and lined with trees but now the main street lined with shops. The small barrel-roofed building on the left at the far end is the island prison built in 1856.

Beyond is **Le Manoir**, built by the first Seigneur and bearing the de Carteret arms, where in 1581 his son presided over the first meeting of the islanders and created the Sark Court of law and legislature.

St Peter's Church dates from the 19C. The embroidered hassocks are the work of the island women; the designs incorporate the motifs and some of the names of the landholdings with which the seats are traditionally associated.

La Seigneurie★ – The present beautiful stone and granite manor house, the residence of the Seigneur of Sark, stands on the site of St Magloire's 6C monastery, after which the house is named La Moinerie. Begun in 1565, it was considerably enlarged in 1730 by the Le Pelley family who then held the fief of Sark. The square tower, which provides a splendid view of the island, was built as a signalling tower in 1860.

The house is sheltered from the wind by a screen of trees and high walls. The **gardens**, on which the Dame of Sark lavished so much attention, are luxuriant with flowers and shrubs, some brought from

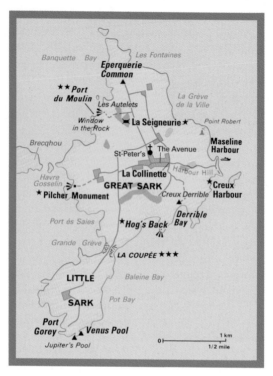

foreign parts, and maintained with undiminished care.

Port du Moulin** – A road along the north side of the Seigneurie grounds soon turns into a path following the windings of the clifftop. The sign "Window and Bay" marks the way to the **Window in the Rock**, which the Revd William Collings had made in the 1850s to provide an impressive **view** of Port du Moulin. *Return to the fork in the path and take the other branch to Port du Moulin.*

The bay, which is popular with bathers in summer, is flanked by stark rocks in strange shapes; at low tide huge arches in the rock appear. On the right stand **Les Autelets**, three granite columns accessible as the sea retreats.

Derrible Bay – At Petit Dixcart turn left into a stony path, then right into a path beside a field; a left fork leads down through the trees to Derrible Bay which a retreating tide will reveal to contain a large sandy beach.

Part way down, a turning to the right leads to the **Creux Derrible**, an enormous hole in the granite cliffs *(take care in poor light)*.

Return to the first fork and bear left, for at the seaward end of this

Pilcher Monument★

This granite column was raised in memory of a London merchant, F Pilcher, who died at sea in 1868 with three companions while returning to Guernsey. From the plinth there is a fine **view** of the west coast and of Brecqhou, Herm, Jethou and Guernsey. A path runs down to Havre Gosselin where yachts moor in the summer months.

high ridge known as the **Hog's Back★** stands an ancient cannon, from which there is a magnificent **view**: to the left Derrible Bay and Derrible Point; to the right Dixcart Bay with La Coupée and Little Sark in the background.

La Coupée★★★ – The concrete roadway and the guard rails were constructed in 1945 by German prisoners of war working under the direction of the Royal Engineers. The narrow isthmus joining the two parts of Sark is uniquely impressive, as on either side steep cliffs drop some 260ft into the sea. The view is magnificent: to the right lie Brecqhou, Jethou, Herm and Guernsey; to the left the coast of Jersey can be made out before the more distant shadow of the French coast. At the foot of the cliff is Grande Grève Bay, a good place for bathing.

Little Sark

On the southern headland are the chimneys of the old silver mines, now overgrown, which were started in the 19C but had to close because of the infiltration of water into the workings. A footpath to the left of the old mine chimney runs down to **Venus Pool**, a circular pool under the cliffs, formed by the sea and visible at low tide.

At low tide *(to avoid being stranded, check the time of high tide)*, visitors can walk from the Venus Pool westward round the headland via **Jupiter's Pool**, several caves and the rocks in Plat Rue Bay, to **Port Gorey** which served the silver mines.

The clifftop path is always open and provides a fine view down into Port Gorey. ∎

HERM

Population 97
Michelin Atlas p 5 or Map 503

Herm (1.5mi long by 0.5mi wide) lies half-way between Guernsey and Sark. The broad sandy beaches on its north coast contrast with the steep cliffs at the southern end of the island. Herm is a haven of tranquillity having neither roads nor cars; walking is the only way to enjoy the profusion of wild flowers, the dunes, the trees and cliffs. The deep fringe of rocks which lies offshore is most impressive at low tide.

Southwest of Herm, across a narrow channel, the islet of Jethou *(private property leased from the British Crown)* rises like a hillock in the sea, the home of many sea-birds.

Historical notes – Prehistoric tombs made of granite slabs found in the north of the island are evidence of human settlement in 2000 BC; little remains, however, of a Roman presence other than a few coins and some pottery. In the 6C Christianity was introduced by St Magloire who founded

Herm Harbour

monasteries in Sark and Jersey. The monks of Sark built a small chapel on a reef between Herm and Jethou, but this was engulfed in the 8C during a violent storm which separated the two islands. In the 17C pirates used the island as a base from which to prey on the many shipwrecks in the area; it was later deserted until the 19C when, for a brief period, granite was quarried for export.

As Crown property the island has been leased to various tenants: in 1890 a German prince, Blucher von Wahlstatt, built the manor house and planted the pine and eucalyptus trees; in 1920 Sir Compton Mackenzie settled there and wrote several novels on and about the island, including *Fairy Gold*, before finally settling on Jethou. During the Second World War the island was occasionally occupied by German troops and appeared in a German propaganda film called *The Invasion of the Isle of Wight;* in February 1943 the British mounted a commando raid. In 1947 Herm was sold by the Crown to the States of Guernsey and in 1949 Major Peter Wood and his wife became tenant. In 1987 the lease was transferred to their family company to enable their daughter Pennie and her husband Adrian Heyworth to become the guardians of the island. During the 50 years of family tenancy the island has been carefully developed for the needs of tourism while at

the same time the peacefulness and outstanding natural beauty have been maintained. There is a small permanent community of 10 families living and working on Herm throughout the year.

■ Tour of the island *3hr*

Le Manoir Village – A surfaced road climbs up to the farm and the handful of cottages which make up the hamlet next to the 18C manor house with its square tower.

Practical Information

Tourist Information Centre – www.herm-island.com
Island Office, Herm Harbour, Herm. Open daily, 8.30am-5.30pm. ☎ 01481 722 377

Where to Stay and Where to Eat –Overnight accommodation is available at the White House Hotel (☎ 01481 722 159), 18 self-catering units (☎ 01481 722 377) and Seagull Campsite (☎ 01481 722 377). Daily visitors are catered for by the Mermaid Tavern and two restaurants in the hotel.

Local specialities – Look for Herm oysters and mussels on the menu.

Access – By boat from St Peter Port, Guernsey *(see 111)*. The boat docks at the harbour jetty at high tide but at low tide at the landing steps at Rosière.

Herm Trident – Weighbridge Clock Tower Kiosk, St Peter Port: ☎ 01481 721 379; Fax 01481 700 226
Catamaran service from Guernsey to Herm (20min): Operates (weather permitting) daily.

Shopping – Island gift shops.

Walking – There is a network of scenic footpaths running round and across the island.

Beaches – The best beaches are at the north end of the island.

St Tugual's Chapel was built of island granite in the 11C when Robert the Magnificent was Duke of Normandy. There is a handsome stained-glass window depicting Christ stilling the Tempest.

The Common – The northern end of the island is composed of sand dunes, known as the Common, covered by prickly vegetation and fringed by sandy beaches which are very popular in summer (Bear's Beach, Mousonniere Beach, **Shell Beach** so called because it is composed of millions of shells deposited by the tides and currents from the Gulf Stream). Half-way along the north coast stands a stone obelisk which replaces the menhir that mariners once used as a landmark.

Le Grand Monceau★ – From this hillock there is a splendid panoramic **view** of the sands, the rocks and the islands. North on the horizon lies Alderney; to the east the French coast. **Le Petit Monceau** beyond is a smaller hillock, overlooking the Bear's Beach.

The Cliffs – In contrast with the low land in the north, the southern end of the island is composed of steep granite cliffs dropping sheer into the sea. In **Belvoir Bay** nestles a small sheltered beach, good for bathing. The southern headland, **Sauzebourge Point**, provides a view of Jethou *(southwest)* with Guernsey in the background *(west)* and Sark *(southeast)*. ■

PRACTICAL INFORMATION

See also pp 25, 58, 88, 100 and 106.

■ Planning a trip ■

Documents – Holders of British and Irish passports do not require passports or entry visas to enter the Channel Islands. Nationals of other EU countries require ID cards only. Nationals of non-EU countries need visas, and should clear customs when entering the UK.

Health – It is essential that all personal travel insurance should include the cost of medical treatment and eventual repatriation; the Channel Islands do not extend the facilities of a free National Health Scheme to visitors from the rest of the United Kingdom.

Jersey has reciprocal health agreements with the United Kingdom and the Isle of Man, whereby residents of these countries are entitled to immediate necessary medical treatment free of charge at the General Hospital in St Helier. Charges are made for non-emergency treatment and for treatment provided by General or Dental Practitioners.

Domestic Animals – There are **quarantine regulations for domestic animals** arriving from anywhere other than Great Britain; no animals from elsewhere are allowed to land in the Guernsey Bailiwick (Guernsey, Alderney, Sark and Herm); Jersey will accept animals under strict controls; for details apply to Emeraude Shipping Line or Jersey Tourism *(see below and p 25)*.

Time – The Channel Islands follow the same time as the UK: British Summer Time (BST) in summer, Greenwich Mean Time (GMT) in winter.

Special Needs

Many of the sights described in this guide are accessible to people with special needs. The **Michelin Red Guide Great Britain and Ireland** indicates hotels with facilities suitable for disabled people; it is advisable to book in advance.

Money – The local **currency** is Sterling: Bank of England notes and coins are freely accepted. Both Jersey and Guernsey have their own coins and notes which are not legal tender outside the Channel Islands but the notes can be exchanged, free of charge, at HSBC, Lloyds TSB and Natwest in Jersey, at banks in the UK.

All the major UK clearing **banks** are represented on Jersey and Guernsey (closed Saturday and Sunday): most cash points are situated at the airports or in town (St Helier and St Peter Port). There are no cash points on Sark and Herm. Cheques drawn on a UK bank are widely accepted if supported by a valid bank card. All the major credit cards are also widely accepted.

Postage – Each Bailiwick issues postage stamps for use in its own area: rates to the other islands, the British mainland and to the Continent vary.

Telephone – Each Bailiwick issues telephone cards for use in its own public phone boxes; they are available from the Tourist Information Centre, petrol stations, newsagents and other shops. Telephone calls to the UK require the same STD codes as apply on the mainland.

Certain mobile networks require a roaming facility; this should be checked with the supplier.

Emergencies – Dial 999 and ask for the service required: fire, ambulance, police.

■ Getting there ■

Access by Air – Direct to Jersey and Guernsey from most airports in the UK by the companies listed below. Direct to Alderney from Southampton and Guernsey. There is also an inter-island air service operated by Aurigny Air Services *(see below)*.

Aer Lingus – www.aerlingus.com
☎ 0645 73 77 47 (from the UK); ☎ 01 705 3333 (from Dublin)

Aurigny Air Services Ltd – www.aurigny.com
☎ 01481 822 886; Fax 01481 823 344; res@aurigny.com; admin@aurigny.com
Services to Guernsey from Manchester, London Stansted and East Midlands, from Dinard and Amsterdam; to Alderney from Southampton – passport required at check-in; restricted luggage allowance of 15kg per bag, with excess charges for heavier items.

British Airways – www.britishairways.com
☎ 0845 77 999 77 (enquiries); 0845 77 333 77 (reservations)
Services from Bristol, Edinburgh, London Heathrow, London Gatwick, Manchester, Newcastle, Paris, Plymouth, Southampton, Dublin

British European – ☎ 08705 676 676; Fax 01392 366 669; marketing@british-european.com
Services from Aberdeen, Belfast City, Birmingham, Bradford, Dublin, Edinburgh, Exeter, Glasgow International, Isle of Man, Leeds, London City, London Gatwick, London Luton, Southampton

British Midland – www.flybmi.com; www.britishmidland.com
☎ 0870 607 0555, ☎ 0345 554 554 (reservations), ☎ 00 44 1332 854 854 (from outside the UK); Fax 01332 854 105
Services from Belfast, Birmingham, East Midlands, Edinburgh, Glasgow, Leeds/Bradford, Liverpool, Teesside

Brymon Airways – www.Britishairways.com
☎ 0845 77 333 77
Services from Bristol and Plymouth

Manx Airlines –www.manx-airlines.com
☎ 08457 256 256; enquiries@manx-airlines.com
Services from Cardiff, Isle of Man, Cork, Dublin

VLM Airlines – www.vlm-airlines.com
☎ 020 7476 6677; 020 7476 6427
Services from London City

Access by Sea – There are ferry services from Poole, Weymouth (high-speed catamaran) and Portsmouth in the UK and also from Ireland. Average travel times are Poole to Guernsey 2.5hr then 1hr to Jersey before returning to Poole via Guernsey; Weymouth to Guernsey 2hr; Weymouth to Jersey 3hr 15min; Portsmouth to Alderney 3hr. Tide conditions will determine whether vessels dock first in Jersey and then in Guernsey or vice versa: check at time of boarding.

Sark and Herm are served by boat from Guernsey *(see pp 100 and 106)*.

Condor Ferries Ltd – www.condorferries.co.uk
Condor House, New Harbour Road, South, Poole BH15 4AJ
Weymouth Quay, Weymouth DT14 8DX
☎ 0800 735 3333; ☎ 0845 345 2000 (Poole reservations);
☎ 01305 761 556 (Poole port arrival information);
☎ 01305 761 551
☎ 01534 872 240 (24hr info line);
☎ 01534 601 000 (Jersey port enquiries);
☎ 01481 729 666 (Guernsey port enquiries);
☎ 00 33 299 200 300 (St Malo port enquiries)

Irish Ferries – www.irishferries.com; info@irishferries.com
2-4 Merrion Row, Dublin 2 ☎ 0990 17 00 00, 08705 17 17 17, 01 638 3333
(reservations, 01 855 2222 (head office)
Ferryport, Alexandra Road, Dublin 1 ☎ 01 661 0511
Rossslare Harbour ☎ 053 33158

Stena Line – www.stenaline.co.uk
Charter House, Park Street, Ashford TNB24 8EX ☎ 0870 570 7070; Fax
01233 202 361, 01233 202 231; info.ie@stenaline.com

Sea connections with France include services from Carteret (Portbail), Dielette and Granville and a fast ferry from St Malo.

Emeraude Lines – www.emeraud.co.uk; sales@emeraud.co.uk
St Helier, Jersey Channel Islands JE2 3NW
Jersey ☎ 01534 766 566; Fax 01534 768 741
Guernsey ☎ 01481 711 414; Fax 01481 715 272
St Malo ☎ 02 23 180 180; Fax 02 23 181 500;
Granville ☎ 02 33 50 16 36; Fax 02 33 50 87 80;
Carteret/Dielette ☎ 02 33 52 61 39; Fax 2 33 53 51 57

■ Motoring ■

Motoring – Hire cars are available in Jersey, Guernsey and Alderney. Private cars (maximum width 7ft 6.5in) may be taken to Jersey and Guernsey. No cars (private or hired) are allowed on Sark and Herm.

No **caravans** or mobile homes are allowed in the Channel Islands. Exception may be made for vehicles specially equipped to carry disabled people but permission must be obtained in advance (☎ 01534 725 511 Jersey Planning and Environment Department).

For **parking and other regulations** see pp 25 and 58.

■ Where to Stay and Where to Eat ■

It is advisable to book well in advance for the holiday season.

Booking Service – Most local Tourist Information Centres operate an accommodation booking service, both inside and outside their area, for those who prefer to tour freely and are happy to make last-minute arrangements.

Hotels – There is a full range of hotel accommodation from the most expensive and formal to smaller and more modest establishments. Accommodation guides are available from Tourist Information Centres.

Guesthouses – Some guesthouses are similar to small hotels but less formal and with fewer public facilities; others are more like bed and breakfast accommodation. Individual addresses are available from specialist accommodation guides and from Tourist Information Centres.

Bed and Breakfast – A directory of carefully selected B & B addresses for London, Great Britain and Ireland is published by

Bed and Breakfast (GB) – www.bedbreak.com
94-96 Bell Street, Henley-on-Thames RG9 IXS
☎ 01491 578 803; Fax 01491 410 806; bookings@bedbreak.com

Self-Catering – A popular alternative is self-catering accommodation – a holiday cottage, a farmhouse, a remote stone cottage, a wing of some Romantic castle, a narrowboat or horse-drawn canal barge. Information available from the local Tourist Information Centres.

Details of privately-owned properties, which have been inspected and listed under four categories – approved, commended, highly commended and de luxe – by the West Country Tourist Board, are published in its own *Inspected Holiday Homes*.

Hostels – Youth hostels in the United Kingdom are open to members of the Youth Hostel Association or holders of an international membership card. Package holidays are available comprising youth hostel vouchers, rail and bus pass or hostel vouchers, return rail fare and cycle hire.

Youth Hostels Association – www.yha.org.uk
Trevelyan House, Dimple Road, Matlock, Derbs DE4 3YH ☎ 0870 870 88 08 (Customer Services), 01629 592 600; Fax 01629 592 702; customerservices@yha.org.uk

Useful Publications – The **Michelin Red Guide Great Britain and Ireland** is an annual publication, which presents a selection of hotels, guesthouses and restaurants. All are classified according to the standard of their amenities, and their selection is based on regular on-the-spot visits and enquiries. Pleasant settings, attractive decor, quiet or secluded locations and a warm welcome are identified by special symbols.

The places listed in the Michelin Red Guide Great Britain and Ireland are underlined in red on the **Michelin map 503** (scale 1:400 000 – 1in = 6.3mi), which also covers Wales, and in the **Michelin Motoring Atlas Great Britain and Ireland**.

Hotels

JERSEY

Moorings – Gorey Pier, Gorey, JE3 6EW; ℡ 01534 853633; reservations @themooringshotel.com £58-£136. Located at the base of Gorey Castle, overlooking the waterfront, once the heart of the oyster fishing industry. Well-priced; the first floor bedrooms have terraces. Pleasant decked area at front of restaurant.

Panorama – La Rue du Crocquet, St Aubin, JE3 8BZ; ℡ 01534 742429; info@panoramajersey.com £45-£106. Personally-run hotel with conservatory, garden and bay views. Also boasts a teapot collection. The superior style bedrooms are very pleasant. All rooms boast good amenities.

Harbour View – Le Boulevard, St Aubin, JE3 8AB; ℡ 01534 741585; info@harbourview.je £33-£80. Relaxed little hotel with authentic feel; harbour front position. Large decked terrace area. Colourful rooms. Simple, rustic menus with many regional flavours.

Sabots d'or – High St, St Aubin, JE3 8BZ; ℡ 01534 43732; sandralecorre @yahoo.co.uk £28-£60. Traditional floral furnishings in homely and cosy bedrooms. Well located for shops, watersports; its cobbled high street position not far from picturesque harbour. Homemade desserts a dining room highlight.

Porthole Cottage – La Route au Moestre Market Hill, St Aubin, JE3 8AE; ℡ 01534 745007; portcott@itl.net £35-£67. Brick and stone guesthouse overlooking St Aubins harbour; shrub-filled, elevated rear garden. Nautically inspired breakfast room with beams and galley window. Cottagey rooms.

Eulah Country House – Mont Cochon, St Helier, JE2 3JA; ℡ 01534 626626; eulah@jerseymail.co.uk £185-£230. Spacious Edwardian country house near St Helier with views of St Aubins Bay. Stylishly combined lounge and breakfast room. Superior quality rooms highly designed.

GUERNSEY

Maison Bel Air – Le Chene, Forest, GY8 0AL; ℡ 01481 238503; juliett e@maisonbelair.com £39-£57. Welcoming peach and white guesthouse; overlooks Petit Bot Valley with shady, peaceful, south facing garden. Comfortable rooms; ideal base for touring the island.

La Michele – Les Hubits, St Martin, GY4 6NB; ℡ 01481 238065; lamichel ehotel@ukgateway.net £38-£10. Painted and clapboard façade with conservatory lounge and secluded garden. Lovely seating area around the pool. Fermain bay is nearby; pleasant, unfussy bedrooms.

La Frégate – Les Cotils, St Peter Port, GY1 1UT; ☎ 01481 724624; c.shar p@lafregatehotel.com £95-£175. Kaleidoscopic views of harbour life and St Peter Port to be savoured from large windows in most bedrooms at this charming hillside hotel. Peaceful location; friendly staff. Stylish restaurant with lovely terrace.

ALDERNEY
Farm Court – Le Petit Val, St Anne, GY9 3UX; ☎ 01481 822075; relax@farmcourt-alderney.co.uk £42-£84. Converted stone farm buildings around cobbled courtyard and garden. Sitting room and breakfast room. Spacious well-appointed bedrooms with contemporary and antique furniture.

HERM
White House – Herm, GY1 3HR; ☎ 01481 722159; hotel@herm-island.com £78-£198. Hotel with real country house feel: offset by verdant hills, the beach extends to the door. Guernsey and Jethou can be viewed from the hushed lounge. Attractive rooms. More formal conservatory with seafood emphasis.

Restaurants

JERSEY
Bistro Soleil – La Route de la Haule, Beaumont, JE3 7BA; ☎ 01534 720249; £14.75-£29.50. Series of connected rooms with superb views over St Aubins Bay. Minimalist style: just a couple of modern pictures. Freshly prepared, bold menus with Mediterranean accent.

Jersey Pottery (Garden Restaurant) – Gorey Village, Gorey, JE3 9EP; ☎ 01534 851119; jsypot@itl.net £19.50-£29.40. Unusual restaurant in working pottery with displays of earthenware, hand-decorated pots in dining room. Tasty seafood dishes. Impressive patisserie counter. Charming setting.

Suma's – Gorey Hill, Gorey JE3 6ET; ☎ 01534 853291; £18-£34.75. Cheerful, contemporary restaurant; terrace from which to enjoy fine views. Detailed food is innovative in its design and the enjoyment is enhanced by pleasant service.

Green Island – St Clement, Green Island, JE2 6LS; ☎ 01534 857787; greenislandrestaurant@jerseymail.co.uk £21.25-£25.25. Lovely location on the beach; coir carpeted, nautically fitted restaurant with wide ranging, daily changing menu at affordable prices. Welcoming, casual atmosphere.

Borsalino Rocque – La Rocque, JE3 9FF; ☎ 01534 852111; £9.10-£29.50. Well-spaced tables in large conservatory and dining room filled with curios. A long-established family business, popular with island residents. Wide choice in menus.

Frere de Mer – Le Mont de Rozel, Rozel Bay, JE3 6AN; ☏ 01534 861000; £10-£33. Dine alfresco with the sea breeze on your face and panoramic coastal views. Menus with strong fish base and good blackboard special alternatives. Classic style and service.

Old Court House Inn – St Aubin's Harbour, St Aubin, JE3 8AB; ☏ 01534 746433; ochstaubins@jerseymail.co.uk £19.95-£35.50. Atmospheric quayside inn, once a courthouse and merchant's house, dating from 15C. Bar featured in Bergerac TV series. Cosmopolitan menu with seafood emphasis. Neat bedrooms (£40-£120).

La Capannina – 65-67 Halkett Pl, St Helier, JE2 4WG; ☏ 01534 734602; £12-£32.50. A buffet display of seafood and Parma ham preside over airy dining room with prints of Venice and Pisa. Choose between Jersey fish and Italian pasta. Dessert from the trolley.

GUERNSEY

Fleur du Jardin – Kings Mills, GY5 7JT; ☏ 01481 257996; info@fleurdujardin.guernsey.net £17-£24.75 Daily menus of local seafood give this granite 15C inn a standing of quiet renown. Cosy interior: rough hewn walls, alcoves, stone fireplace. Smart, sizeable rooms (£79.50-£106).

The Auberge – Jerbourg Rd, St Martin GY4 6BH; ☏ 01481 238485; theauberge@cwgsy.net £25-£28. A splendid spot to sample worldly flavours in brasserie-style dishes with excellent views of sea and islands. Seafood predominates amongst fine game and meat options.

Café du Moulin – Rue de Quanteraine, St Peter in the Wood, GY7 9DP; ☏ 01481 265944; vincentfam@guernsey.net £20-£35. Delightful converted 19C granary with terrace and gardens in country setting. French chef concocts thrilling combinations: lobster and mango salad, braised Burgundy snails.

Le Nautique – Quay Steps, St Peter Port, GY1 2LE; ☏ 01481 721714; £14.50-£29. On the quayside overlooking main harbour; offers mix of French inspired seafood and meat dishes. A variety of fish features, to be grilled with the sauce of one's choice.

Saltwater – Albert Pier, St Peter Port, GY1 1AD; ☏ 01481 720823; info@saltwater.gg £18.70-£26.95. Warmly run restaurant in impressive location at end of historic pier overlooking harbour near large marina. Modern feel. Extensive menus have a solid seafood slant.

L'Escalier – 6 Tower Hill, St Peter Port, GY1 1DF; ☏ 01481 710088; armelleetdean@hotmail.com £17-£44.50. Carefully designed restaurant with an appealing sheltered terrace and attentive service. Good value, quality dishes utilising seasonal ingredients and island produce.

Zest – Lefebvre St, St Peter Port, GY1 2JP; ☏ 01481 723052; £14.50-£27.45. Hidden away in town centre with homely décor and intimate semi-boothed seating. Wide-ranging, good quality dishes with a modern base: menus are frequently changed.

ALDERNEY

First and Last – Braye, GY9 3TH; ☎ 01481 823162; £13-£29. Positioned by the harbour with scenic views. Simple pine furniture, blue cotton tablecloths. Nautical theme prevails. Keen use of island produce with seafood base.

SARK

La Sablonnerie – Little Sark, Sark, GY9 0SD; ☎ 01481 832061; £23.80-£28.80. Former 16C farmhouse; a long low building with gardens. Diners greeted from jetty by Victorian horse and carriage. Home-produced ingredients flavour the cuisine. Simple rooms (£59.50-149.50).

Fitz's – Rue Lucas, Sark GY9 0SD; ☎ 01481 832302; fitzs@gtonline.net £24-£33. Simple eatery in cosy street; snug, homely style décor prevails. Small bar; dining is at black ash tables. The classically based dishes use mainly island ingredients.

■ Further reading ■

For reference...

The Model Occupation: The Channel Islands Under German Rule, 1940-1945 by Madeleine Bunting (Pimlico 2004)

The War in the Channel Islands: Then and Now by Winston G Ramsey (After the Battle 1989)

Balleine's History of Jersey by G R Balleine (Phillimore 1998)

...and for pleasure

Last Ditch by Ngaio Marsh (Harper Collins 2001)

John Nettles' Jersey: A Personal History of the People and Places by John Nettles (Tiger 1992)

INDEX

Director	David Brabis
Series Editor	Mike Brammer
Editor	Alison Hughes
Picture Editor	Éliane Bailly, Geneviève Corbic
Mapping	Michèle Cana, Alain Baldet
Graphics Coordination	Marie-Pierre Renier
Graphics	Antoine Diemoz-Rosset
Lay-out	Alain Fossé
Typesetting	Sophie Rassel and Franck Malagie (NORD COMPO)
Production	Renaud Leblanc
Marketing	Cécile Petiau, Hervé Binétruy
Sales	John Lewis (UK), Robin Bird (USA)
Public Relations	Gonzague de Jarnac, Paul Cordle

Special Thanks: Jon Combe

Contact Michelin Travel Publications
Hannay House
39 Clarendon Road
Watford
Herts
WD17 1JA
United Kingdom
☎ (01923) 205 240
Fax (01923) 205 241
www.ViaMichelin.com
TheGreenGuide-uk@uk.michelin.com

MICHELIN
Travel Publications

Hannay House, 39 Clarendon Road.
Watford, Herts WD17 1JA, UK
www.ViaMichelin.com
TheGreenGuide-uk@uk.michelin.com

MANUFACTURE FRANÇAISE DES PNEUMATIQUES MICHELIN
Société en commandite par actions au capital de 304 000 000 EUR
Place des Carmes-Déchaux – 63 Clermont-Ferrand (France)
R.C.S. Clermont-Fd B 855 200 507

Published in 2004